THE MAN
IN THE
SYCAMORE
TREE

THE MAN IN THE SYCAMORE TREE

The good times and hard life
of Thomas Merton

An Entertainment, with photographs
by Edward Rice

A Harvest/HBJ Book
Harcourt Brace Jovanovich, Publishers
San Diego   New York   London

Grateful acknowledgment is made for the use of excerpts from the following material:

MY ARGUMENT WITH THE GESTAPO by Thomas Merton. Copyright © 1969 by the Abbey of Gethsemani, Inc. Copyright 1968 by Thomas Merton. Reprinted by permission of Doubleday & Company, Inc. THE SEVEN STOREY MOUNTAIN by Thomas Merton. Copyright 1948 by Thomas Merton; THE SIGN OF JONAS by Thomas Merton, Copyright 1953 by The Abbey of Our Lady of Gethsemani, renewed 1981 by The Merton Legacy Trust. Both reprinted by permission of Harcourt Brace Jovanovich, Inc. ASIAN JOURNAL by Thomas Merton © 1973 by The Trustees of the Merton Legacy Trust. Reprinted by permission of New Directions Publishing Corporation. EMBLEMS OF A SEASON OF FURY by Thomas Merton. Copyright © 1963 by the Abbey of Gethsemani, Inc.; FIGURES FOR AN APOCALYPSE by Thomas Merton. Copyright 1947 by New Directions Publishing Corporation. Both reprinted by permission of New Directions Publishing Corporation. THE NEW MAN by Thomas Merton. Copyright © 1962 by Farrar, Straus & Giroux, reprinted by permission of Farrar, Straus & Giroux. ORIGINAL CHILDBOMB by Thomas Merton. Copyright © 1962 by The Abbey of Gethsemani, Inc.; RAIDS ON THE UNSPEAKABLE by Thomas Merton. Copyright © 1966 by The Abbey of Gethsemani, Inc.; THIRTY POEMS by Thomas Merton. Copyright 1944 by Our Lady of Gethsemani Monastery. All reprinted by permission of New Directions Publishing Corporation. THOMAS MERTON by Irving and Cornelia Sussman. Copyright © 1976 by the authors, reprinted by permission of Macmillan Publishing Company. THE WAY OF CHUANG TZU by Thomas Merton. Copyright © 1965 by The Abbey of Gethsemani, Inc.; ZEN AND THE BIRDS OF APPETITE by Thomas Merton. Copyright © 1968 by The Abbey of Gethsemani, Inc. Both reprinted by permission of New Directions Publishing Corporation. Previously unpublished material by Thomas Merton, Copyright © 1970 by The Trustees of the Merton Legacy Trust.

Printed in the United States of America

Library of Congress Cataloging in Publication Data

Rice, Edward.
    The man in the sycamore tree.

    Reprint. Originally published: Garden City, N.Y. : Doubleday, 1972.
       1. Merton, Thomas, 1915-1968. 2. Trappists—United States—Biography. 3. Monks—United States—Biography. I. Title.
BX4705.M542R5 1985   271′.125′024 [B]   84-22490
ISBN 0-15-656960-4
First Harvest/HBJ edition 1985
A B C D E F G H I J

THE MAN
IN THE
SYCAMORE
TREE

It yawns at me the cavernous gulf.
Find, find the nuns and make them pray.
De ore Leonis, libera nos Domine: and
      again, De manu canis unicam meam.
Hand of the dog reaching out
      from under fur, lousy false dog.
What is to be done?
Miserere.

All the goats, all the dogs, all the
      blank cattle, all the brute cattle, all
      the horned cattle, all the snarl,
all the fake,
all the bellow,
all the monster,
one horn, one man's foot,
one beast's claw, one hen's eye,
one yak's tooth,
one of everything mister,
one of everything.

These are my opinions of today's cosmos.
St. Giles, defend
              us.

UNPUBLISHED LITANY

He WAS AN Aquarian, born January 31, 1915, and died in the early days of the Aquarian Age, under the sign of the Archer, Sagittarius, who had struck him down with a bolt from the heavens (disguised as a faulty wire), in Bangkok, the gilded city of the kingdom of the Thais. "Two days after Thomas Merton's death," wrote an American who had attended the conference where Merton had died, "four not very large alligators living in the *klong* [canal] came out onto the grass. There, in sight of the monks, including Dom Rembert [Weakland, O.S.B., the Benedictine Primate], one of them seized and killed a dog." He continues: "It seemed strange to me in retrospect to recall that in an Indian parable about the inevitability of death, the form taken by the god of death to complete his mission was that of an alligator."

Aquarius: "Honest, probing, broad-minded, amiable, humane, popular."

Again: "Idealistic, artistic, intellectual, honest, easily influenced, popular yet solitary, often abnormal." Ending on the anniversary of Thomas Merton's entry into the monastery, that is, December 10th, his life fell almost exactly into two parts. He was six weeks short of being twenty-seven when he left the secular world, and was exactly twenty-seven years a monk of the Abbey of Our Lady of Gethsemani the day of his death in 1968. He would have been fifty-four on his birthday.

He was buried with appropriate ceremony in Gethsemani, after his body had been brought back to Kentucky by a U. S. Air Force plane, a fitting tribute to a pacifist who had not only opposed the Vietnam war, but even World War II and had spent his adult life an active and outspoken enemy of all wars.

And the alligators. There is said to be a tradition (at least among some . Buddhists) that when a Buddha is reincarnated on earth he will not be recognized until his death. We will know that a Buddha has been among us when alligators come and eat a dog. And now certain Buddhists believe that Merton was a reincarnated Buddha. And as a Buddha? After leaving America, Merton went first to Bangkok and then to India

Merton in his "Hemingway" phase: the man of action and daring, as he thought of himself at the time he wrote THE LABYRINTH. This is the photograph he enclosed with the manuscript. The time is summer 1939.

to visit various Tibetan refugee lamas, among them the Dalai Lama and other holy men. From Calcutta he told Bob Lax, half joking, half seriously, that the lamas thought he was some kind of Buddha. "Is everywhere jovial Lamas who acclaim me the chenrezigs and the reincarnation of the Dops of Lompzog or the Mops of Jopsmitch." "I am discovered to be the mahayana bootstrap attempting to escapt from its own bottle." And while I was writing these notes, I visited Bramachari, the Hindu monk who was a close friend of Merton's at Columbia in the late 1930s, and upon meeting him (we were in East Bengal, in a remote Hindu village in the Ganges delta,) I was struck by his resemblance to Merton. Bramachari was in the midst of offering puja, or worship, to the Lord God Shiva, which he performed with the same quick, definite gestures which were also Merton's. He had become stocky, his head was shaved; his eyes were clear and sharp. For a moment his face and build made him seem almost like Merton reincarnated. Later in the day the resemblance was less pronounced, though it never faded.

*

It is one of the tragic facts of life that the world often needs the death of a man before it realizes the value of his life and work. Merton had been with us a long time—his first poem after becoming a Trappist monk was published in *The New Yorker* in 1942—and it was easy to dismiss him as the "talkative Trappist." The obituaries in the general press didn't seem to grasp the point of his life: in them *The Seven Storey Mountain*, his autobiographical work which recounted his early life and premonastic years, and his life as Trappist up to 1948, when the book was published, was the end, not a beginning. What more could a monk say who had voluntarily abandoned all communication with the rest of mankind? What he wrote later, they indicated, was redundant or irrelevant and superfluous. *The New York Times* put him in his place

by saying, "For some avant-garde Catholic intellectuals Merton was partly stranded in the medieval-garde.... Even when Merton wrote about the justice of demands by Negroes, or the injustice of duties imposed by governments, he seemed a far echo of the message that was clear to others before him."

The truth is the opposite. His early writings are good and important, and if we had them alone and his purely religious works (making allowances for a certain seventeenth-century Cistercian harshness that runs through some of the first ones and for some hasty theology in others, which he apologized for later), we would still judge Merton as a seminal writer of the Catholic Church in the twentieth century, even in those that reflect the temper of another, pre-Conciliar period. It is the later writings, on war and peace, nonviolence, race, on ordinary life, on giants and titans, and above all on Buddhism, that show Merton at his best and most creative. And most revolutionary. One doesn't always need a bomb or an underground to bring down the world: a word can do it, and the word was there, slowly altering the consciousness of many of us. "He changed my life," one person after another said about him, a remark that was made even near the end at Calcutta, where he attended a conference of world religions.

The two main themes in Merton's later life were peace—in various forms: social and racial justice, freedom, love, liberty—and the interior life, and neither excluded the other. It is interesting to see these themes develop over the years; almost everything he wrote was connected with one or the other. Merton saw nonviolence as the logical corollary of the Kingdom of God. In a beautiful essay he wrote the year before his death, he pointed out that the Christian nonviolence is built on the basic unity of man. The nonviolent resister is fighting not for himself but for everybody. Merton summarizes a point that Gandhi had made, that "the fully consistent practice of nonviolence demands a solid metaphysical and religious basis both in being and in God." And then he develops this same theme as it applies to the Christian, pointing out what we all know and forget, that the Christian message is for all men and not for the individual alone who preaches it.

He was intensely practical about the search for peace. I remember a cold January morning when we drove around the Kentucky hills in one of the Abbey's pickup trucks while he talked about the self-immolators who were setting themselves on fire; he expressed his concern that not only were such actions personally wrong but they distracted people from the real work to be done, and turned others against the peace movement. He could also be bitter and sarcastic in making a point. In "Chant to Be Used in Processions Around a Site with Furnaces," one of his unsettling straightforward horror poems, after developing the theme that the commander of the death camp had all the while been merely following orders in getting people into the gas chambers, which he did with efficiency, dispatch and even a touch of humor ("they would be given a greeting card to send home taken care of with good jobs wishing you would come to our joke") and boasting that "In my day we worked hard we saw what we did our self-sacrifice was conscientious and complete our work was faultless and detailed," he concludes by saying, "Do not think yourself better because you burn up friends and enemies with long range missiles without ever seeing what you have done." On another occasion, he wrote: "Yesterday I offered Mass for the new generation of new poets, the fighters for peace and for civil rights, and for my own novices. There is in many of them a peculiar quality of truth that older squares have rinsed out of themselves in hours of secure right-thinking and non-commitment. May God prevent us from becoming 'right-thinking men'—that is to say men who agree perfectly with their own police."

Needless to say, his other great interest, Eastern religion, in which Buddhism was his special field, complements his work on peace. This interest goes back as early as 1935, when he first read Aldous Huxley's *Ends and Means*, along with a series of Buddhist texts in French edited by Father Léon Wieger, S.J. He saw Buddhism not as a substitute for Christianity but as an enrichment and a fulfillment. He was not tempted, as other Christian writers on the East have been, to pick out plums for decorating Christianity, but regarded Buddhism as a viable way into which the Christian could enter without compromising his own beliefs. Merton repeatedly stressed that Buddhism was a *way*. In an essay on Zen Buddhist monasticism, he attributes the great popular interest in Zen in the West to the "widespread dissatisfaction with the spiritual sterility of mass society dominated by technology and propaganda, in which there is no room left for personal spontaneity." He appreciates the "frank thoroughgoing existentialism and dynamism of Zen," which he sees as a "philosophic and existentialist type of spirituality, capable of bringing man into an authentic confrontation with himself, with reality, and with his fellow man." In another essay he talks of Zen's "metaphysical honesty." He did not however accept Buddhism without qualifications, realizing that it needed "a radical renewal of the Buddhist experiential grasp within the framework and context of a bitter, agonizing social struggle, and in terms that are comprehensible to those who are most deeply involved in that struggle. This formula applies not only to Buddhism but to every religion that seeks to find its real place in the world of today." However, he pointed out that Zen Buddhism offers us "a phenomenology and metaphysic of insight and consciousness that has extraordinary value for the West." And it was in search of those insights and consciousness of the Buddhist way that he met his death.

"I was overwhelmed with sadness, sitting at the end of the row, because I suddenly remembered all the times I had sat in movie houses at the beginning of the afternoon, waiting for the picture to start."

THE MAKING OF
A BEATNIK, PEACENIK
TRAPPIST BUDDHIST
MONK

His LIFE was often one of nostalgia, alienation and loneliness. He wrote: "I remember all the nights I was ever awake, in France, when I was a child.

"The windows of the Lycée's infirmary looked out over the tiled roofs of a suburb in Montauban. There was a white wall, that already looked destroyed, between the Lycée and the street. Over there, somewhere, southward, on the edge of the yellow bluff this part of town stood on, was the small Gothic spire of a new church, overlooking the small square full of stunted plane trees where they guillotined the murderers from the town's prison. Beyond that, the bluff fell to the plains where the Tarn River ran. Out there was emptiness, wood smoke, vineyards, the dark and violent night, the house of the bishop, the barracks of the African troops.

"And from those barracks, a fierce, outlandish Islamic bugle would blow, so that I shivered, where I lay in my infirmary bed. I used to lie awake and listen to the sounds of the South of France outside that bare window, and beyond the ruined wall. A distant train, beyond the river, shrieking with its high-pitched and forlorn whistle. Far off in the town a harshly clanging church bell that rings rapidly and stops all of a sudden, in some brick tower. . . .

"All around me, from that ward, in the infirmary, spread the Lycée in every direction in long brick wings two stories high. In these were some dormitories, part empty (for the place was only half full), part full of iron beds where lay the peasant children of the South in their tough sleep, lean, hard, mean kids full of violence, strange humor and rhetoric."

And in England, where he was boarded out with family friends while his father was dying of a brain tumor: "There was a lot wrong with this orphan. Of course, he wasn't strictly speaking English. As a matter of fact, he wasn't really British, either; it was by no means certain you could call him a thorough colonial. He was showing signs of too many bad Con-tinental traits, a kind of French sullenness, perhaps treacherousness, a kind of Spanish haughtiness, a kind of Italian indolence." The Frobishers, the family which was caring for him, suspected him of secret rebelliousness. Mrs. Frobisher gave him a lecture: one's duty is to run with the pack. "Hunt with the group. Everybody depends on everybody else. Everybody does his bit." The lecture continued with horrible examples. "Then I went out of the house with my book in my hand and dived through the laurels and climbed into a small cedar with roomy branches where you could sit and read comfortably. And there I read how the Count of Monte Cristo, tied in a sack, hiding inside with a knife, was thrown for dead over the high bastions of the Château d'If into the sea."

I have been quoting from *My Argument with the Gestapo*, the book Merton wrote in 1941, and not from *The Seven Storey Mountain*, his autobiography. The first book is quite personal and subjective, the latter, even with the highly developed ratiocinations and introspective meditations, is more objective. In the first, we know what the young Merton *felt*, his alienation and loneliness. *My Argument with the Gestapo* tells us a lot about Merton's childhood, not the American periods but those in France and England. And it says even more about his sense of estrangement from the world, particularly in those very nostalgic, very alienated descriptions of London.

"In how many strange rooms in London have I awakened and lain in bed, sometimes loving the pale sun in the window, sometimes loving the smell of tea on the stairs, sometimes loving the sound of water running into a bath, or the sight of the Christmas fogs; but how much oftener have I awakened to hate the blackness of the days, the wet wind stirring the sooty curtains, the voices of the foreigners on the stairs, and the sound of water weeping in the confinement of air shafts on which my window opened.

7

"Behind the silences of the city's great restraint are clearly heard the voices of all the great dark areas of the slums, the recriminations of hundreds of slowly dying regions full of low, narrow houses and smoke and tears. And then there are heard the gaiety of the doomed and their terrible resignation.

"And all around are heard the whisperings of the doorways and the cynicisms of the mews where the whores live, and the thin, cheating euphemisms of the family hotels, the dark resignation of the prisons and the muffled strangled wit of the law courts, the grave, coy antics of the librarians and the essayists, and the old men in the museums." When he walked the streets of London at night, "I learned to listen to the gaiety of the taxi drivers turn to ashes, the harlot's curse, and the dead good humor of the crippled beggars who lie to amuse the rich, and the servile obscenity of the songs they whisper in the corners of the bars, with the toothless humanism of their laughter and the good, staunch equalitarianism of their blasphemies." London was "as dark as chaos, as inescapable as Fear."

Yet there were also many warm, enjoyable periods in his life when he was with his parents and later his grandparents. Merton's parents had met in Paris. His father, Owen Merton, was an artist from New Zealand; his mother was an American, and her parents, Pop and Bonnemaman, lived in Douglaston, Long Island. Merton was born in Prades, which is a beautiful little village in the French Pyrenees. When he was a year old, his parents moved to America and got a house in Flushing, Long Island, then a rather quiet and provincial town, not far from Douglaston. Here, in 1918, his brother, John Paul, was born. Three years later—Merton would have been six— his mother went to the hospital with cancer. Meanwhile, life had been rough for the Mertons: his father had to struggle to support them, working at night playing the piano in a movie house in Bayside and as a gardener during the day. After a few days in the hospital Mrs. Merton wrote her older son that he would never see her again. "I took the note out under the maple tree in the back yard, and worked it over, until I had made it all out, and gathered what it really meant. And a tremendous weight of sadness and depression settled on me. It was not the grief of a child, with pangs of sorrow and many tears. It has something of the heavy perplexity and gloom of adult grief, and was therefore all the more of a burden because it was, to that extent, unnatural. I suppose one reason for this was that I had more or less had to arrive at the truth by induction."

Owen Merton was a wanderer: when possible he took the children with him, to Provincetown and Bermuda, where they lived briefly. Eventually he returned to Europe, leaving the children with Pop and Bonnemaman. In 1925, Owen Merton was sufficiently at ease to bring his sons to France to live. Merton didn't like the idea at all: "Why should anyone want to go to France?" he thought. When all his objections were useless, he burst into tears. But Owen Merton calmly went ahead with his plans. The Mertons traveled a lot in western Europe, occasionally meeting Pop and Bonnemaman, and the boys went to school in France, boarding at a lycée, and after two years they moved to England: more schools and shifting around. John Paul was sent to Douglaston to live with his grandparents and Merton went to Oakham. a boarding school in Scotland. And his father became ill, very ill, and was confined to the hospital, and here, after many months of suffering, he died. There was a trip home —which was now Douglaston—in the summer of 1931, another rather longish year at Oakham and then Merton took the Grand Tour to Italy. He had just turned eighteen.

In Rome he began to discover something of the Christian past, the great churches with their impressive frescoes and mosaics. He was fascinated by Byzantine mosaics and began to haunt the churches and chapels where they were to be found. It suddenly struck him that the Church represented Christ, was Christ, the "Christ of the Apocalypse, the Christ of the Martyrs, the Christ of the Fathers . . . the Christ of St. John, and of St. Paul, and of St. Augustine and St. Jerome and all the Fathers—and of the Desert Fathers. It is Christ God, Christ King . . ." He said: "So far, however, there had been no deep movement of my will, nothing that amounted to a conversion, nothing to shake the iron tyranny of moral corruption that held my whole nature in fetters. But that also was to come. It came in a strange way, suddenly, a way that I will not attempt to explain.

"I was in my room. It was night. The light was on. Suddenly it seemed to me that Father, who had now been dead more than a year, was there with me. The sense of his presence was as vivid and as startling as if he had touched my arm or spoken to me. The whole thing passed in a flash, but in that flash, instantly, I was overwhelmed with a sudden and profound insight into the misery and corruption of my own soul, and I was pierced deeply with a light that made me realize something of the condition I was in, and I was filled with horror at what I saw, and my whole being rose up in revolt against what was within me, and my soul desired escape and liberation and freedom from all this with an intensity and an urgency unlike anything I had ever known before. And now I think for the first time in my whole life I really began to pray—praying not with my lips and my intellect and my imagination, but praying out of the very roots of my life and my being, and praying to God, the God that I had never known to reach down towards me out of His darkness and to help me to get free of the thousand terrible things that held my will in their slavery."

*

HE WAS IN LOVE often, with all kinds of girls, English, American, Middle European. He mentions a number of

them, vaguely, and his own "selfish" treatment of them in the autobiography. There was one he talked about a lot later at Columbia, a girl he knew while at Cambridge. His relationship with her resulted in a head-on confrontation with his guardian in London. "The thing that made me suffer was that he asked me very bluntly and coldly for an explanation of my conduct and left me to writhe. For as soon as I was placed in the position of having to give some kind of positive explanation or defense of so much stupidity and unpleasantness, as if to justify myself by making it seem possible for a rational creature to live that way, the whole bitterness and emptiness of it became very evident to me, and my tongue would hardly function." When the summer recess came, Merton took the boat to New York, and here he received a letter from his guardian suggesting that he give up Cambridge and that it would be very sensible to stay in America. But the girl was very much on Merton's mind. From time to time he talked about returning to see her, but he was never able to go back to England, and the girl and her son were killed in the Blitz. No one can recall all the details today, and there is no need to speculate on them, except to say that it was a serious, complicated situation and in retrospect clearly one that had a lot to do with his eventual conversion and vocation.

In February 1935, Merton entered Columbia College, commuting there from Douglaston, where he still lived with his mother's family. Columbia was in a chaotic state at that time, reflecting both its own internal dissensions and the national and international scene. It was late in the depression, and the rise of Fascism deeply concerned many students. There were antiwar demonstrations ("NO MORE WAR!" and "BOOKS NOT BATTLE-SHIPS" and many left-wing demonstrations and tiny right-wing ones) and a continuing campaign to reinstate a student named Bob Burke, who had clashed with Nicholas Murray Butler, the

Campus demonstrations were common during Merton's period at Columbia. The most important centered around a protest against the university's acceptance of an invitation to celebrate the five hundredth anniversary of Heidelberg, Germany. Students staged a Nazi-type book-burning in protest, and one of the campus leaders was expelled. Demonstrations continued for months afterward, with the university winning in the end.

Merton was art editor of JESTER, the campus humor magazine. He is seated at the left, with Bob Lax (center) and Ralph de Toledano at the editors' desk. JESTER was called "a noisy boiler room" because of the constant parties, fires in wastebaskets and intra-office squabbles over editorial policy and fights with the magazine's business department.

At campus hangouts and fraternity house parties Merton drank a lot and sang bawdy songs ("The Bloody Great Wheel" and "The Good Ship Venus" were songs he was noted for). He is also said to have introduced a collection of British and Australian limericks to the campus. The standard drinks at the time were muscatel and beer. Merton is at the far left in the top photograph.

Although he was at Columbia for only two years, Merton soon became "A Big Man on Campus," being involved in various publications, sports, dance committees, secret societies and other activities. Above: He is seen with a group of fraternity brothers.

The official class picture shows Merton as a rather baby-faced young man. In the photograph below he is lined up with a group of classmates on a geology field trip in eastern Pennsylvania.

Wearing a watchchain and society badge, Merton poses expansively in the Columbia quadrangle. This photograph and those on the preceding pages were taken from the COLUMBIAN, the yearbook of which he was editor.

president of the university. But what was most tragic was the underlying rot which became more and more apparent. Eugene Williams, who was managing editor of *Jester* (Merton was art editor), finally wrote a cogent, and pained analysis of Columbia, which states in part: "Columbia's educational crisis is making it a queer and unstimulating place to live and learn in." [Williams was twenty at the time, a thin, intense and extremely intelligent person. He later committed suicide.] He added in his charge: "Within the memory of this melancholy observer Columbia College has been a lively and exciting place ... with good writing and good talk.... Thinking on the campus was mostly adolescent and fruitless, but it excited controversy and made educations—and there was plenty of it.

"All that is gone now. By the grace of God knows what besides the Admissions Office, Columbia has become supernally dull, and in many things more important than football this is the worst we have seen....

"Political action is nearly dead.... The American Student Union sleeps through threatening depression and inevitable war, mass meetings on South Field attract only the tiniest of masses, and the campus cops have nothing more serious to distract them than the occasional noisy construction of a mobile in the *Jester* office. On all sides there is a stink of decay, unrelieved by one heartening belch of talent or spirit."

But Merton had found Columbia exciting. "Compared with Cambridge this big sooty factory was full of light and fresh air. There was a kind of genuine intellectual vitality in the air—at least relatively speaking." He threw himself into campus life with a tremendous energy, joining a fraternity, Alpha Delta Phi, temporarily trying out for the crew and for the cross-country team. He was editor of *Columbian*, the college year book and art editor of *Jester*. He also wrote for the campus newspaper and the literary quarterly, and did reviews for *The New York Times*. In the middle of the day and after classes he would come to the fourth floor of John Jay Hall, which was where campus activities were centered, the varsity show, the glee club, the chess club, *Jester*, *Spectator*, and other publications, and the athletic office. Often he went into the varsity show rehearsal room where there was an old upright piano. One day, after I first began to submit drawings to *Jester*, amid all the confusion of the fourth floor, I heard an incredible, noisy, barrel-house blues piano drowning out everything else (my first impression of Merton was that he was the noisiest bastard I had ever met), like four men playing at once. "Who is the crowd playing piano?" I asked. "Only Merton," said Gene Williams. Merton soon came bustling into *Jester*. He was always full of energy and seemed unchanged from day to day, cracking jokes, denouncing the Fascists, squares, being violently active, writing, drawing, involved in everything. He was invariably dressed like a businessman, in a neat suit and a double-breasted chesterfield topcoat, carrying a leather briefcase full of papers, articles, books and drawings. Noisy. Authoritative. Sure of himself. But behind it all was that relentless, restless search to find himself, to learn who he was.

In *The Journal of My Escape from the Nazis* (published after his death as *My Argument with the Gestapo*; I prefer the original title), which in effect is the search expressed in allegorical terms, he kept posing the question. "If you want to identify me," he says to the British officers who are questioning him, "ask me not where I live, or what I like to eat, or how I comb my hair, but ask me what I think I am living for, in detail, and ask me what I think is keeping me from living fully for the thing I want to live for. Between these two answers you can determine the identity of any person. The better answer he has, the more of a person he is.... I am all the time trying to

make out the answer as I go on living. I live out the answer to my two questions myself and the answer may not be complete, even when my life is ended I may go on working out the answer for a long time after my death, but at least it will be resolved, and there will be no further question, for with God's mercy I shall possess not only the answer but the reality that the answer was about." (The officer rolls his eyes in despair.)

One day Ralph de Toledano said: "Hey, Rice, aren't you a Catholic?" I was, sort of.

"Merton wants you to be his godfather." Cynical attitudes among everyone else at *Jester*, and along the fourth floor. The only other known Catholic was a kid who gave an interview to *Spectator* defending Franco and letting his running nose drip into a dirty snot-green handkerchief. Merton went to see Father George B. Ford, the Catholic chaplain for the campus. I thought Merton was crazy, not that I had strong opinions one way or the other. Father Ford assigned him to Father Moore, one to submit drawings to *Jester*, amid all the Christi, for instruction. "I was never bored," said Merton, "I never missed an instruction, even when it cost me the sacrifice of some of my old amusements and attractions, which had had such a strong hold over me and, while I had been impatient of delay from the moment I had come to that first sudden decision, I now began to burn with desire for Baptism, and to throw out hints and try to determine when I would be received into the Church." Finally, on November 16, 1938, he was baptized, with me, Bob Lax, Bob Gerdy and Seymour Freedgood in attendance.

About nine years later, when I was getting married, I went to see Father Ford. We began to talk about Merton. "He's the third Collyer brother," said Father Ford. "There's a bit of the Collyer in everyone of us. Tom happens to have to have it in the extreme." I told Father Ford that I thought Merton was entitled to his own way of life, but Father Ford was adamant: Merton should have stayed in the world and played an active role.

*

THOSE OF US who weren't in politics (far left, of course) went off, vaguely, without guru or guide, into half-baked mysticism. Merton seemed to be the only person who talked sensibly to Bramachari about religion. Bramachari suggested that instead of trying to find solutions in the East, that Merton look into the great Western spiritual works like St. Augustine's *Confessions* and *The Imitation of Christ*. But others of us were dabbling in the *Ignatian Spiritual Exercises* and at the same time carrying around a book called *Witchcraft, Magic and Alchemy*, full of occult knowledge, and magic circles and formulae for calling up the devil, and thirdly, Patanjali's *Yoga*. *The Spiritual Exercises* were mildly interesting, not because they were Christian but because they hinted at an interior voyage; however, they were never tried because they demanded so much self-discipline and an end to teen-age dissipation. No one dared attempt the devil calls, because, well, he might respond. Patanjali's *Yoga* taught a process of psychological discipline and a knowledge of the self and the soul by which man could gain both release from earthly misery and from the circle of transmigration through the heavens. But we were all deeply committed to worldly involvement. Bramachari, who really didn't want to preach or convert, had an effect on no one but Merton (and perhaps Lax and Seymour), and at one of Freedgood's New Year's Eve parties (which Merton said was otherwise rather dull), John Slate tried to tie up Merton with Bramachari's beautiful yellow and red cotton prayer turban.

Lord Jagad-Bondhu, the Hindu saint whose cult Bramachari introduced to Lax and Freedgood, sits in the lotus position. Merton found a copy of this picture pinned to the wall in Lax's room where he and Freedgood threw knives at it.

Merton photographed Rice and Lax against the background of the Allegheny Mountains. (Rice looks hung over.) On another occasion, Merton and Lax. dressed in their Sunday best, sit on the porch of Benjy Marcus's cottage, where they were living during the summer of 1939.

OLEAN I. We are in Olean, in Benjy Marcus's summer cottage in the hills overlooking the city. Benjy is the husband of Gladys, Lax's sister Gladys, whom everyone calls Gladio. He is a pudgy, middle-aged, affable businessman, who with his brothers owns a hotel, the Olean House, where we collect our mail, and he has something to do with oil; to the south are the first oil fields to be discovered in America, around Oil City and Bradford, right on the Pennsylvania border. On a clear day one can hear the whump, whump of the oil machinery. The cottage is in the Allegheny Mountains, overlooking a series of wide gentle hills and valleys, thickly crammed with pines and oaks. The air is clear; in the days the sun is hot but the nights are cool. The cottage is big, with a nice porch on which we put a trapeze. Lax's relatives and friends hang around, including one who is a jazz musician. Benjy has a collection of "pornographic" literature which he smuggled out of France and into America, including Henry Miller's *Tropic of Cancer*, the unexpurgated *Lady Chatterley's Lover*, and some other books. He also has Evelyn Waugh's *Vile Bodies*, and *Decline and Fall*. Merton and Lax tell me about Donne, Blake and Rabelais, and get into terrific arguments about St. John of the Cross and are annoyed with each other. There is a wild man up the road who is said to have killed a woman and hidden the body. One day we hear a shot and all fall on the floor. Merton puts a hat on a stick and holds it up at the window. No more shots. We grow beards and we are insulted by the Oleanders when we go to town to collect our mail and buy food and see a movie. Almost immediately we decide to have a novel-writing race, the winner to be the person who writes the most pages in five days. Merton works very seriously on a very autobiographical book, called at first *Straits of Dover*, then *The Night before the Battle* and finally *The Labyrinth*. Lax's is about a traveling night club and is *The Spangled Palace*, and mine is *The Blue Horse*, which is

about a race around the world. We sit at our typewriters in the big living room (it is too cold and rainy to go outdoors the first few weeks), glowering at each other and trying to estimate the number of pages the other fellows are turning out. From time to time we go half a mile down the mountain to a bar called Lippert's, where we drink a lot of beer and play the piano and drums. Merton has more money than Lax and me, and buys bottles of scotch and the novel-writing contest begins to deteriorate. Lax and I give Merton glasses with orange peels and sugar, and Merton becomes very drunk, laughing and singing; the next morning he awakes feeling fine and remarks, "No hangover. Shows the advantage of drinking good scotch." We finish our books eventually, desultorily, and also keep journals, which are combinations of diaries, comments, observations, lists of anything—friends, books, movies, furniture, ideas, hopes and fears. Life is simple, but there is an interior tension, as if we are trying to break out of something. We are, but are unable to formulate it. We drink, go to Bradford where we are cleaned out by a confidence man at a carnival, pick up girls from the TB sanitarium down the road, drink, get arrested. Lax's cousin Bob Mack, who likes big flashy cars and flashy blondes, comes up to see us, with a cigarette hanging from the corner of his lip, like a French working man. The food is terrible. My journal records that we are eating waffles for breakfast (which comes at noon), waffles for lunch, which is in the evening. Merton makes hamburgers soaked in scotch. They are so bad (we are eating outdoors) that he takes them all and throws them over the roof of the house one after another like baseballs and tries to throw the peas after them singly. Fried ham sandwiches; gin in grapejuice; malnutrition. Not liking the food but hungry all the time. Hungry. We play jazz records by the hour: Bessie Smith, Armstrong and King Oliver, Bud Freeman and Jess Stacey, Bix,

Seymour Freedgood, one of Merton's closest friends, liked to appear mysterious and daring. He lived in a world of deep, dark secrets and undercover acts, which nobody, particularly Seymour, took at all seriously.

Teschmacher, Pops Foster. Although we are potted, absolutely potted all summer, it is, by today's terms, a rather simple and uncomplicated existence. Naive.

Then Merton and I are back in New York. He goes to graduate school at Columbia and teaches a few courses in English at night and I return to college. Lax remains in Olean and works as an announcer at the local radio station. Merton's and my novels are turned down by various publishers. *The Spangled Palace* appears in *Jester*, which I edit, as a serial and eventually Bob Gerdy and I rewrite it as a musical comedy. *Jester* contains largely the work of the editor's friends, who to a man are fighting the Establishment and are young, rebellious, alienated misfits and (in their own eyes) downtrodden and poor. World War II has started, the depression is not yet over and the future is unpromising. There is a lot of heavy drinking and parties that never seem to stop, rushing about in cars and trains and buses. There is also a lot of talk about marijuana, which is called muggles, reefer, tea, charge, mezz, eagle dust, gauge, mary jane and mary warner, stick and weed ("A friend with weed is a friend indeed"). Lax is legendary because he is known to have smoked reefers when he lived under the roof of Furnald Hall on Broadway with Seymour Freedgood and Bramachari, the Hindu monk they had adopted. (It was against regulations to let nonstudents sleep in the dormitories, but Bramachari made himself invisible when the cleaning women came into the room.) Joe H. sends me muggles from El Paso in a shoe polish tin; one can also get a high on terpin hydrate with codein. There are endless dates with impressionable young Barnard girls, more sober, less angry than we are; Merton, now deeply involved with the Church, seems tolerantly amused because he is growing into another world. There are rumors also (and he sometimes hints this) that he is about to get married.

The year passes. Instead of marrying, Merton becomes more and more involved with the Church; he works on his thesis, he teaches. The world is crazy, war threatens, one has lost a sense of identity: the adolescent crisis is there, but delayed because, not having television or *Mad*, we mature later. People are dropping out: Tommy F., vaguely seen people. The rest of us are lost. We read *Look Homeward, Angel* and send each other postcards saying, "O lost!" But Merton has already zeroed in: the Church is a living vital reality. God is immanent. We are in different worlds. We meet, talk about writing and drawing (he contributes poems and drawings to *Jester*), drink (but he is becoming careful), have meals. Merton has a deepening interior life, while the rest of us are—where?—scattered like good and bad seed upon good and bad ground. Six friends try mass suicide: they jump into the Hudson while drunk but the tide is out and they return with muddy trouser legs. Basically we are healthy and will survive, many of us, but we pay in our way. And Merton in his, as we will see.

*

OLEAN II. The second summer at Olean is far livelier, hectic. There are many more people, coming and going and wandering about. Besides Lax and Merton and me, there are, at one time or another, Jim Knight, Seymour Freedgood, Robert Gibney, Bob Gerdy, Ad Reinhardt, Nancy Flagg, Peggy Wells and some other girls, one of whom is named Norma Prince, who tacks a canvas on the wall to paint a nude of Walt Whitman; the canvas isn't large enough, so she continues the painting right over the edges and onto the wood paneling, irritating everyone. We are having coffee in the Olean House, me, Merton and Knight and Norma Prince; Merton makes some jokes about girls with mustaches. In horror we glance covertly at Norma; there is a heavy down on her upper lip. Lax, Knight and I set up another novel-writing race. Knight writes a beautiful, sad Wolfean prose (he is from Georgia), full of interior suffering and loaded with southern angst, Lax something about a circus family, which goes through years of transmigrations and

After graduating from Columbia, Merton lived in the balcony apartment on Perry Street in New York's Greenwich Village. For a long period after he became famous, this house and Our Lady of Guadalupe Church on Fourteenth Street (as well as Columbia) were part of the "Merton Tour" that his readers took.

"Jeepers Creepers, cried Tom, the Fun-loving Rover. . . ."

Merton was an accomplished and witty artist; he drew with facility and speed. The cartoon above was one of a number in JESTER; he had a similar series, slightly more risqué, in a magazine published by the Dixie Cup Company. The drawing of the man in the beard accompanied an article on beards in Rice's year of JESTER. The running women, the nudes and the calligraphic drawings were done in 1940 and 1941, while he was trying to make up his mind about the religious life.

PLES SIT STRAIT

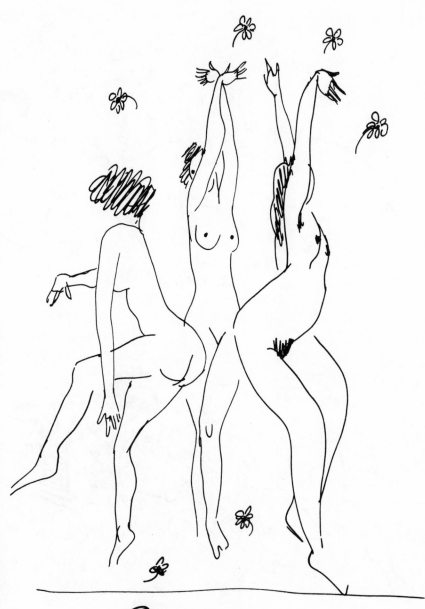

Primavera.

The Foot race.

tm.

The Soldier's gure!

DAME WINNING A LOTTERY.

Come on, ziggy! Be a sport! give me a cigar! We're prepared! Hey! Thank you folks! Hey! Thank you folks!

Come on, sport! Come on, slugger, wake up! we're home!

Be happy! Zip! Zip! Come on. He's vomiting, the beer made him sick!

Zip! Zip! Get in the boat! look at dogface! He's vomiting, the beer made him sick!

Zip! Zip! Zip! Zip! Hey dogface! Zip! Zip! Zip! Zip! Zip! Hey dogface! Zip! Zip! Zip! Heard any dirty jokes? Some Zip! Hey Scotty!

Zip! my son! Hey dogface! Hey! Ethel, look at dogface! He's vomiting, the beer made him sick!

Come on soldier. Zip! Zip!

PATRIOTIC
SINGER.

Come on, soldier! Hey! Zippy! Let's have 3 Rays for Uncle Zammy! Old Zip! Zip! Come on whip you whip Heinrick Hitler! Come on soldier. Zip! Zip! hold your coat while you whip Heinrick Hitler!

One-two-Zip! Let's all trust Frank! Let me hold your coat while

Merton decorated his passport photo (taken for
his trip to Cuba) with glasses, hair and beard.
This was at a time when he was infatuated with
beards, putting them in almost every drawing.
The inscription below is on the reverse of the
photograph and shows his interest in
portmanteau words.

Nobody hardly
can recognise
mir, after the
wunderbare
hair geschöpf
treatments I have
attended lately.

eventually appears as *Circus of the Sun*, and I, a book called *Keep Your Distance, Mr. Baxter*, about some musicians and gangsters. Knight and I get our heads clipped almost to the bone. A few days later Lax and I have ours shaved, on the spur of the moment. Gibney draws a face on the top of Lax's, which upsets Freedgood in the depths of some ancestral taboo about painting the flesh. The cottage is so crowded that some of us move to the car shed. Freedgood comes in one night while we are sleeping and writes on the wall in black crayon: "Salvation by suicide," and "VANIS IN NOTITIIS SAEPA INCENTUR ERROR ET HAERESIA," and "Better dead than costive."

On the road. We are restless. We move back and forth into Olean, hitchhiking, taking a taxi, bullying Bob Mack to get us in his big touring car. Gerdy, Knight, Merton and I decide to go to Cleveland where Gerdy has relatives, one of them "rich." We split up, Gerdy and me, Knight and Merton. Rides are scarce; I finally shave my beard which seems to be scaring the farmers, and eventually we all meet in Shaker Heights. Knight and I hitch back to Olean without incident, but Gerdy and Merton are forced to take the train. I hitch to New York with Seymour, he to see his wife, me to see my girl who is working as a mother's helper in Rockville Center, Long Island.

Yoga. One lies down & takes 23 long deep breaths, expelling every possible bit of air and then filling the lungs again to the greatest possible expansion and holding the 24th breath. This gives a fine sensation of calm and rest, with soft colors floating before the eyes, blues and soft dark yellows and greens, the latter coming in a haze.

Nightmares. Merton spends the greater part of one night talking to us in his sleep in an unintelligible language and laughing wildly. ("Perhaps the things I remember in nightmares are the things everybody is really fighting for," he writes later in a novel.) Seymour sees a ghost and runs through the french doors. Living

conditions: suspicion of fleas, malnutrition is rampant. We get a cat from the supermarket. There is always someone eating, someone shitting, someone sleeping, someone cooking, someone typing, drawing, chopping wood, rattling dishes, pouring coffee; all this in the cottage, and when the water runs out, half of these things are prevented or hindered, and the other half go on in greater force. Food. We eat pork chops for three days straight. (On July 23 I note in my journal: What we forgot to buy yesterday in town was food for today. Now we will have to have gin and wine for supper. A full four weeks later I note: For about three days or perhaps more we have been drunk, either on wine or beer, or gin, a party all the time, for all the fellows.) Norma Prince plays Boer records; she has brought or sends for Bix, Cuban, African and Whiteman records. A man from the Department of Health comes to get a sample of the water. "It's a miracle to me why he didn't complain of the squalor we live in, a week's dirty dishes, a month's dirty sheets, rotten food spread all over the kitchen and the dining room, garbage lying on the floor, the sink thick and stopped up with grease, torn newspapers, magazines and odd scraps of old drawings and pictures and manuscripts strewn about the house. When I was home my father complained about a spot on the kitchen floor and made me wash the floor on my hands and knees under penalty of cutting off my allowance. Before I went to see Fannette I didn't mind the dirt so much; it was too hard to clean up, and all you had to do was to move to a less dirty place until that was too filthy and then move again. But coming back here, after living for ten days in a very clean house I was disgusted to think that we have been living in this mess without being bothered by it. Now I am used to it again." Mary, the Polish cleaning woman who comes here on Friday nights, says there are plenty of dirtier houses in Olean [I think she was being kind to us]. They are hard to imagine. There is an awful bad smell in the kitchen that no one can get rid of, especially around the sink. Cockroaches in the kitchen, Merton reports. During July we stay in bed until two or three in the afternoon because it is cold and rainy and no one has built a fire. It is always cold when we get up, and somebody is always playing an old Paul Whiteman record from 1927, like "Mississippi Mud" or "San," and there are people rattling dishes in the kitchen, swearing at the mess on the dinner table from the night before. After breakfast we go back to bed until six or so, get up for more food, and then sit around wondering why we aren't writing or drawing; and after some time at this, go to Lippert's or into town in a taxi to the movies, come back and do a little work, and about four go to bed again. Merton makes the same two tea bags last all summer. On some cold nights everyone drinks tea made from those two tea bags, eating toast made from stale bread roasted in the oven because that was the only way we could eat some of that bread. In times like that we are very hungry and very cold. [My god, it was cold!] Even though we have a roaring fire the house is eternally cold and the only way to keep warm is to stand huddled against the fireplace. The bedrooms, which are shut off from the rest of the house, are always ice cold, damp and often bad-smelling from the dirty blankets and sheets. No one goes into that part of the house unless necessary. It is like one great big southern Mississippi rural slum in the dead of winter. Finally it warms up, and we go swimming in Cuba Lake. Merton often stays behind, sitting peacefully before the porch, looking out into the valley, or he goes into the woods and thinks. He seems to be working something out in his mind. August 25: "This is Sunday morning (or afternoon) but the house is just like a kindergarten on a weekday, everyone busily engaged in some little activity, drawing and coloring, writing, reading books or newspapers, eating milk and crackers, or maybe just scruffing around. But I can't work because of so many

people; the room is too crowded and it is too cold to go outside; the phonograph, which used to be pleasing with only one or two people around, now becomes a base for all the other noises; and the constant shifting about of people becomes as bad as the Columbia study room." [Four days later I went back to New York to stay.]

*

POST OLEAN. Then the summer was ended. We were all dispersed. Merton got a job as an English teacher at St. Bonaventure's College, which was outside of Olean. He was earning $45 per month, plus room and board. Freedgood and Gibney stayed with Lax. Freedgood finished his book about Bramachari except for a final chapter. Lax wrote: "Here it is 11:30 A.M. and Freedgood has been up all night writing, and now he goes to bed, he's been doing that for a week. I keep waiting for him to trip and break in pieces." "Merton has pried the old accounting professor out of his room at Bonas and has also been given a free ticket to the football games." "It's wonderful here with three people: neat, quiet, no more tension, shredded wheat lasts for days, no butter struggle, onions in abundance, Prince's picture which gave us sore throats is all gone away (nailed face down to the shelf of the hall closet), wherever you look there is an empty seat or a flat surface to lie down on."

Merton takes the train to New York to get his tonsils out but the doctors find that the problem is not tonsils, but something with the nose, which they solve with an operation. He talks about the pleasant life in the country—"Up there it is deep in ten feet of snow, and the snow falleth continually. I sleep and work and sleep and work. Anyway it is pleasant that way. No trolls, no subways, no dangerous crazies, no draft officers right this minute, and not one word of war talk from day to day or week to week"—but whenever possible he comes down to the city to buy books or records and see his friends. He is teaching English to kids from the mining and oil towns in Pennsylvania. He says, "I think they would enjoy Beowulf after I point out its close similarity to football." He also taught them *Sir Gawain and the Green Knight* and *Piers Plowman*. "Some books!" was his comment. "Boy, did they cry big Polish crocodile tears when they learned how much reading they were going to get. I think if I go on thus cruel they will pack up their football helmets and go back to the mines. Wait until they try to figure out Chaucer. I think I'll need a bodyguard for the Chaucer lessons." Meanwhile he is debating within himself the great dilemma: to become a priest or to go to Harlem to do social work.

But the question of a priestly vocation was not so simple. Earlier in the year Merton had applied to the Franciscans (their headquarters were in New York, near the Pennsylvania Station) to enter as a novice. He had had some doubts all along: he was looking for a true monastic life, and the Franciscans had gotten so far away from their original way of life that in effect it had completely disappeared. He complained to me that most of the monks did nothing but sit around the game room in the basement and drink Cokes and listen to baseball on the radio. But he was hopeful that he would be able to make something truly monastic out of the life. During the summer he spent a lot of time at St. Bonaventure's. In September, after the crowd in the cottage had broken up, he went down to New York to the Franciscan mother house: he had begun to brood over certain aspects of his past, of his character and way of life, and it occurred to him that the Franciscan superiors knew nothing about him, that the man they saw as an applicant was not the real Thomas Merton. There are many "wicked" passages in *The Seven Storey Mountain* which always have seemed basically very innocent—crushes on girls, the reading of far-out books, his brief flirtation with Communism, some references to heavy smoking and drinking; and after Merton's death a young woman remarked, "He was worldly, I suppose, by some standards, but his worldly ways

certainly pale before the average social life of an American teen-ager today." The teen-age Merton, the Merton of his early twenties, had been as far out as the beat and the hippy. He had an active sex life (he once told me his first experience was with a beautiful Viennese whore he had picked up in Hyde Park; on another occasion he remarked that he had learned Hungarian in bed), and he had an endless number of nubile, compliant girls, about whom he was actually very cagey and reticent. The one he talked about, half boastfully, half regretfully, was the girl in Cambridge.

While he had doubts about his fitness as a Franciscan, he had doubts about the Franciscans as the kind of monastic order he wanted to enter (he was terribly uninformed about the religious life in general). What had attracted him to the Franciscans was "that tremendous and heroic poverty, poverty of body and spirit which makes the Franciscan literally a tramp." But he was trying not to face the uncomfortable fact that twentieth-century Franciscans had become square and respectable and spiritually sedentary. "Without [true] poverty, Franciscan lyricism sounds tinny and sentimental and raw and false. Its tone is sour, and all its harmonies somewhat strained." Then with what Merton told them about his background and in the light of their regulations, the Franciscans felt it the sensible thing to turn him down as a candidate for their order. It was a tremendous blow to Merton. Yet, after a few moments of actual tears, from guilt and frustration, he was able to pull himself together. If he couldn't be a monk formally, he would at least live and think like one. He bought a set of the Roman breviary and began a life of prayer and meditation.

At the same time he continued to write; he kept a detailed journal (most of which was later destroyed) and was working on another novel. He also had the draft hanging over him; he got a temporary deferment because of bad teeth, but the war and the hopeless mess that mankind had created bothered him deep inside.

He put his hatred of war, his suspicions of the military system into his allegorical book, *The Journal of My Escape from the Nazis*. The main character is Thomas Merton, a citizen of "Casa"; he is "about twenty-six, light hair, blue eyes . . . a writer and went to Cambridge, might be a German or a Norwegian. Talks a little like an American. Doesn't smoke, like Hitler; probably doesn't drink, either. Doesn't like Cambridge." The other details too are the Merton we know: son of a New Zealander and an American mother, born in France, educated there and in England, and a graduate of Columbia College. But that is all the Merton we see on the surface. Inside is the eternal search, much more "interior" than in *The Seven Storey Mountain*, more romantic and nostalgic. Merton is still hunting for the man he is destined to be, in the mazes of bombed London and occupied France, where he escapes the Nazis by going right into their midst. The book is heavily influenced by other writers, the chief being James Joyce, who was the most important model for Columbia intellectuals at that time; but Merton had also been reading Graham Greene's entertainment, *Confidential Agent*, which uses both a mythical country and a portmanteau language called entrenationo. He also wrote, when he was first working on the book, that the new Chaplin movie (*The Great Dictator*) had a great artificial language and mentioned a sign on a store that said "Legomo kaj Fruktü." "Some language!" he added. In the book there is also something of the mood and tone of Rex Warner's *The Wild Goose Chase*, which he may not have read. In some ways, *Journal of My Escape from the Nazis* is a skimpy and juvenile book; in others, it is very profound in what it tells us of Merton, his childhood, and his current attitude toward the world. In no other work does his own fear and alienation come so much alive. The word "fear"

turns up over and over, like a litany. He had been through a major shock, his rejection by the Franciscans, and the draft was hanging over him. The war was getting worse and worse, with the Balkan, Russian and Mediterranean invasions, and all the fears we all expressed about the world in flames were very much with him. But it is not a physical fear but a deep metaphysical fear that undermines the chief character. All along he keeps turning to the Church, to God, in both subtle and direct ways, interspersed with a longing for worldly acceptance. The two desires seem to run hand-in-hand. Near the end of the book he writes to one of the other characters: "I proceed in the same old worldly terms. I am so unpublished. I am a kind of a Trappist, in my own way. I am kept so apart from the thirsting imaginations of the public not unintelligent but greedy for such books as I think I want to write (all about God in a new witty and pertinent way, face first through the muck of the reeky civilization we got ourselves stuck with, and out of the other side with double-talk in my hair like a swimmer free of the weeds!) that I am a kind of Trappist." In June of 1941 he showed part of the manuscript to two publishers, but received no encouragement; nevertheless he continued to work on the book and eventually completed it. Ralph Gleason, who went to Columbia and was a friend of Merton, read the book in manuscript. He said later, "What frightened me was the vision which, without his being there, described it exactly as it was. It made an incredible impression on me because within eighteen months of reading it, I was there in London walking down that same Kensington Avenue and into that same underground station." But Merton's agent, in her introduction to the book, when it was published after his death, wrote about the lack of interest among publishers, "It was 1941. How could one interest anyone in a book about an *imaginary* visit to England and France," when we were getting firsthand reports about the Blitz and the Occupation. "To complicate matters, Tom's attitude toward the picture of brave little England and his sharp remarks on such sacred subjects as Allied propaganda were considered at best, puzzling, at worst, downright suspicious."

But time, and the Lord, were closing in on him. He finished the manuscript and gave it to me to hold. There was something more important to occupy him.

In looking back through his *Secular Journal* I find, besides the spiritual anxieties, a tremendous physical restlessness. He was wandering all about the country. We went down to Washington once for no very good reason (drunk, too, I might add), but alone he wandered back and forth between New York and Olean and up to Boston; his major trips were to Trappist monasteries. Even when he went to Cuba in the spring of 1940, it was as a kind of pilgrimage to it as a "Catholic" country. Once Dan Walsh told him about the Trappists in Kentucky, they were continually on Merton's mind. He began to read about them, and finally, he took the train to Kentucky to see the Trappists at Gethsemani in Holy Week, 1941. What he saw was in effect of a decision he had already made. The date is February 4, 1941:

"... Where's my copy of [Castiglione's] *Courtier*? What thief has it?

"Q. How do you know you didn't give it away according to your well known plans of last year, hey?

"A. You said it, how do I know?

"Q. Incidentally, now that we have mentioned the plan you once entertained this time last year, of entering a monastery: how does it look now?

"A. The same. But I think I'd be a Trappist.

"Q. Now you're joking!

"A. You think so?"

But in the summer there was another pull, Baroness de Hueck's Friendship House in Harlem, where he sorted clothes and shoes for the poor. But two weeks later, he went off to another Trappist monastery, Our Lady of the Valley, in Rhode Island, which may have been a rather bland experience, because his *Journal* (the published form was heavily expurgated) mentions nothing of the monastery itself but contains merely meditations and denunciations of the war and of society's ills. There are long blanks in the *Journal*. On November 24th he writes, after returning from still another trip to New York, "I am not physically tired, just filled with a deep, vague, undefined sense of spiritual distress, as if I had a deep wound running inside me and it had to be stanched. . . . The wound is only another aspect of the fact that we are exiles on this earth.

"The sense of exile bleeds inside me like a hemorrhage. Always the same wound, whether a sense of sin or of holiness, or of one's own insufficiency, or of spiritual dryness." Three days later the crisis had reached its head: "Today I think: I should be going to Harlem, or to the Trappists? . . . Should I do the thing I have wanted to do since Spring, write and find out if the things the Franciscans objected to might be passed over by the Trappists?"

This is the closest he ever came to saying there were real and true impediments to an active acceptance in a religious order. There was still that burning desire to remove himself from the world, from the occasion of sin, guilt, lost love, temptations, and to atone for his past. It would be a complete oblation. "I would have to give up *everything*." He was still concerned about being a writer, but decided, "If God wants me to write, I can write anywhere." Going to Harlem, which will be full of confusion (and he adds, he didn't like the idea of working with a lot of girls, a cryptic remark that was never clarified), doesn't seem to mean anything special, though it is a good and reasonable way to follow Christ. "But going to the Trappists is exciting, it fills me with awe and with desire. I return to the idea again and again: 'Give up *everything*, give up *everything!*' " Then he adds, dramatically, "I shall speak to one of the Friars."

Gethsemani, as it looked when Merton first visited it. He called it "the center of America . . . the axle around which the whole country blindly turns and knows nothing about."

He said that because of the prayers of the monks, "the world is spared, from minute to minute, from the terrible doom."

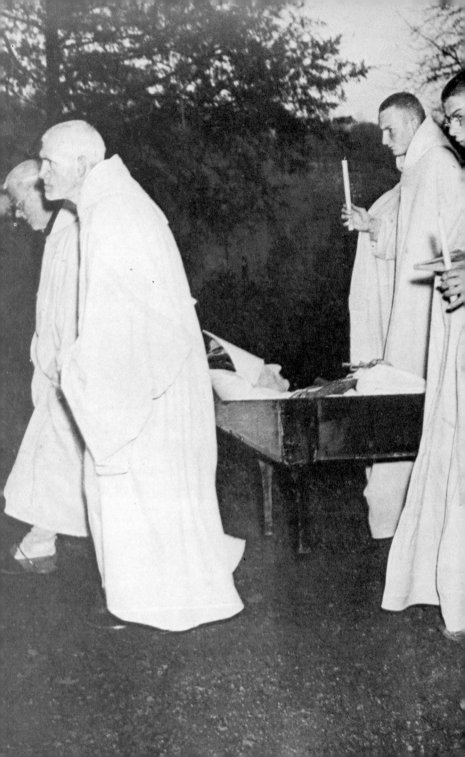

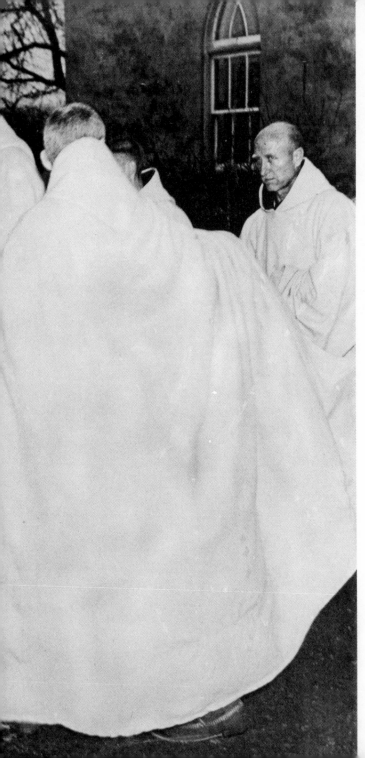

The starkness
and simplicity
of Trappist
life—and a certain
air of
romanticism—
struck deep
into Merton's
evolving
spiritual life.
He liked the
idea that
the Trappists
were stripped
down to the
barest
essentials.
Events, like
this burial of
a Trappist
abbot, touched
him strongly.
But one of his
friends thought
he had gone into
an ecclesiastical
Devil's Island.

Uncle O'remus
Roosevelt
Homer
Wang
Joey Zimmerman
Nestles, Inc.
Happy
Joey the Chocolate King
Jess Stacey
Llwellen
Ottaviani
Frisco Jack
Alban Leixos
Marco J. Frisbee

SIGNATURES FROM MERTON'S LETTERS

GETHSEMANI

It was on December 10, 1941, three days after the bombing of Pearl Harbor by the Japanese, that Merton entered the monastery of Our Lady of Gethsemani, expecting to bury himself within the unimposing gray walls, submitting body and soul to the rigid and demanding discipline of another age. His mind was centered on the Trappist motto, "God Alone," which was painted over the door of the entrance to the old guest quarters, and that, he decided, was to be his only thought. In one of the rare letters that he was allowed to write afterward (the Trappists were given permission to write two at Christmas and two at Easter, and incoming mail was held up until after Advent and Lent), he was enthusiastic and enchanted by the simplicity and austerity of Cistercian life. The letter was written on December 26, barely more than two weeks after entering, and was addressed to all his immediate friends. He begins by saying that his only regret is that he had not entered the previous Easter. He said: "This is the one place where everything makes sense.... Everything that was good when I was a kid, when I was in England, when I was anywhere, has been brought back to life here." And the things that were not good—pride, vanity, arguments, selfishness, ambition, showing off—he found had no place in the monastery. "Everything I wanted to do the most, I can now try to do all the time, without any interference."

When he was in the guest house, waiting to be brought in to the noviate, it seemed strange that he was about to become a Trappist. "As soon as I got inside, I knew I was home, where I never had been or would be a stranger.

"As for this Christmas, I'll tell you it is unbelievable what a holy Christmas God has given us here, or what happiness in Him and in His love, because we belong to Him entirely, we are stripped of the whole world and look for nothing except from His hand, and live in His love and if that is taken away we are less than stones." He added that "We pray all night in tears for the people who are being hit and kicked and killed, and who cannot help it, and there is nothing in the world it is possible for us to be sore at because, literally, if our life ceases to be anything but pure love for one instant we become miserable as stones. Therefore we are sore at nothing but only pray for more love all the time." In a rare letter written before the end of the first year, he told Lax that "It is very good and sweet to be occupied with God only, and to sit simply in His presence and shut up and be healed by the mere fact that God likes to be in your soul." Looking back now at this first year, I suspect that the struggle was even then shaping up. He had already sold a poem to *The New Yorker*, and the creative urge, though stifled could never be eliminated. While he was trying to be very quiet and happy, because he felt that God was very obviously with him, with a presence and a blessedness that he had never imagined possible, there were times when this was clearly not so: he would try to pray or think of Christ, and his mind, instead of filling with peace, was flooded with he-she jokes from *Jester*, slogans, the memories of movies so bad that he had forgotten them previously by the self-protective efforts of the subconscious, only to have them emerge while he was trying to meditate. He thought of million-dollar advertising schemes and wondered why he couldn't concentrate. "The thing that makes most sense," he said, "is to be in the presence of God and live by His will, as we live on air and bread (and to ask Him to make us all be with Him forever)." He became very serious, pietistic and self-effacing: he had jumped wholeheartedly (as in everything) and he accepted without question or qualm whatever his spiritual directors taught. He alternated between states of religious euphoria and emptiness. The interior life could also be bitter, he found, because it was sometimes hard for him to see God doing all the good there is in people, who are incapable of doing

anything in return.

I have not been allowed by Merton's estate to quote directly from the remainder of the letter, but it is worthwhile to go over the subjects he was talking about. He was writing near the end of his first year at Gethsemani, three weeks before the anniversary of his entering. He wrote that because you like God to be in your soul, you also love your neighbor as much as you could by any action of your own: because God cannot be in your soul without having a direct effect on other people, and not necessarily people who have ever heard of you. Because when God is with you, you begin to desire the salvation of distinct

When Merton went through the main gate of Gethsemani, he never expected to go outside again. His sole desire was to remain a cloistered, Trappist monk for the rest of his life, seeing no one but his fellow monks and having no communication of any kind with the outside world.

Trappist life in the early 1940s still resembled nineteenth-century French peasant life. Mechanization had not yet been introduced, the cheese and other businesses, which were to irritate Merton and to draw so much of his scorn and anger, were yet to be developed, and life was simple, direct and very much to the point. Merton threw himself wholeheartedly into the alternating rhythm of manual labor and the Office.

In his first year Merton was pleased to live with "such good monks as all my brothers are." He found that the Rule led men to set aside the harshness and fear he had found in the secular world and to live in charity and joy. He thought that all his brothers were "really saints."

individuals you have never heard of—and to desire it is to obtain it. He obviously had been trying to pass into a nonverbal type of meditation (he apparently succeeded much later), because he makes the point that words are not necessary, though they can be a great joy; other times they are a terrific nuisance. It is plenty, Merton adds, to let God do all that is good. Merton is not too proud to simply enjoy God's kindness, though he is proud enough to be constantly ungrateful for it, and lets himself become concerned with things that are not God's will, or His immense perfection, His joy.

Then in a reference to the past, he states that he didn't come to the monastery to avoid shame at his own weaknesses. His only complaint is that if he were more of a child of God, or a good monk, he would really be glad of his weakness, because it is this that has led God to want to do good for him: for if Merton had not been a sinner, God would not have come to save him. His inability to meditate properly makes him very ashamed and disgusted. He states that this is a trial common to the monastic life, and has good effects, one of the principal ones being that you love God not only for His obvious gifts, but to lead you to realize, by His apparent absence, how infinitely preferable He is to everything else. He explains that this absence is only apparent as is clear from St. John of the Cross, and the other mystics, and the monks at Gethsemani know it perfectly well. When you feel bad in the monastery, it is nothing compared to the bad days you have outside in the world. And as soon as this dryness is done with, your mind unexpectedly fills up with the presence of God, twice as real and twice as holy as before. Another result of these temptations is to make you very docile, very detached from your own opinions and judgment and way of doing things and then you rely on God for the smallest things for everything. This is peace, because God gives everybody everything, and the only reason a person doesn't have

more is that he gets in God's way, trying to get things with our own dumb will. Later on in the letter he makes the point that an important kind of charity in the monastery is keeping the Rule as perfectly as one can, even when it seems silly, because it is the fact of everybody doing things according to the Rule that stops arguments and opposition and fights and leads people to go about quiet and happy. As time went on he was to find out in a very difficult way that the letter of the Rule incorrectly applied was to cause the monks of Gethsemani tremendous suffering and conflict, and that the spirit should have been observed instead.

He continues in a vein that is straight out of elementary works of old-fashioned spirituality, in statements that are not worth repeating today. He was trying to obliterate everything that did not fit into the kind of Cistercian spirituality that he was being taught, or imagined. But what makes these thoughts interesting is that he brings a directness and perspicacity to what is hackneyed and trite and sticky and makes them seem almost fresh. He had, as far as he could, eliminated all extraneous matter from his life, from his mind and soul. It was a complete purging away of the world, and in looking back at this early period, it was obviously necessary for the flood of new ideas, or old ideas freshly and newly seen, that were to enliven him after his ordination. He was critical of the world but not of Gethsemani. He saw the monastery as the "only real city in America," and perhaps he suspended all his critical judgments except when one could not be avoided. He ends on a relatively minor, but indicative, point, with a long passage about the reading at meals in the refectory. He says it is nice to listen to books, even bad books, while he was eating his black bread and oats—not that the books are all bad or all good. Some were very good, he thought, like St. Bernard's sermons on the Canticle of Canticles. He couldn't remember the bad ones, but he added that Franz Werfel's *The Song of Bernadette* was fairly good. Much later he began to tune out on these readings (years afterward he admitted that he was tempted not to like St. Bernard and that when the *Sermons in Cantica* were read in the refectory during his novitiate, he was irritated by the breasts of the Spouse), and eventually he was able to take his meals at his hermitage and avoid them altogether. But in the beginning he was trying to be a *good* monk. A very good one.

*

BUT THE EARLY YEARS were physically hard and rigorous. The monks slept on straw-covered boards in a big dormitory (by 1966 each man had his own comfortable room); the bed was too narrow and too short, and Merton was bothered by the smell of the straw and the very cold room in which they all slept. Day and night they lived in their robes, a light one in the summer and a heavy one in the winter, but there was no heat (the fire in the chapel was not lighted until there was frost on the windows). The fasts were unusually strict and the hours of communal prayer longer than in later years. The food was hardly more than bread and fruit and barley coffee. There was a lot of manual labor: felling huge trees and sawing and splitting them into logs, and work in the gardens and fields and ordinary household chores. He had always worried about his health, and now at Gethsemani he tried not to, even though he would work long hours at manual labor in the cold, and then in his sweat-drenched robes stand shivering in the drafty basilica during the Office. This was a penance for him; he knew it and it still worried him that he was even then concerned about his health when he stood sniffling and sneezing. He considered his chills a penance for worrying about his health. He told himself to be happy that Jesus wanted him to learn to forget about his body and not to let his fears keep him from sitting in the peace and silence of his soul's inner house. He believed that it was hard to be indifferent about what was

happening to his body, but he believed it essential to the pure love of God. But at the end of his novitiate his health broke down; he was taken off hard manual labor and put to translating French books and articles.

*

THE SPIRITUAL MERTON might be dominant, and if so, only by a heroic act of the will, and temporarily, but the creative Merton was never buried. Poems came to him at the most inopportune time, in choir or in meditation, and he received permission to put them down. His thoughts ran along apocalyptic lines (one of his first books was called *Figures for an Apocalypse*), and the same kind of images occur frequently where people escape from the world to meet in "the holy desert," which is the monastic life. One runs:

> I met a traveller from the holy desert,
> Honeycomb, beggarbread eater,
> lean from drinking rain
> That lies in the windprints of rocks.

Another says that:

> More than we fear, we love the holy desert
> where separate strangers, hid in their disguises,
> Have come to meet, by night, the quiet Christ.

He continued to write poems. One of the most touching was his evocation of the death of John Paul, who had joined the Royal Canadian Air Force, and had come to say good-bye to Merton at Gethsemani in the late summer of 1942. John Paul had wanted to be baptized, and Merton crammed him with religious instruction and John Paul was received into the Church. In *The Seven Storey Mountain*, Merton's most poignant and revealing passages concern John Paul. When I knew him, in 1940 and 1941, he was a wild blond kid, tremendously likable and probably further out than any of us. One day he said he had been trying to join the United States Air Force. I asked him what he would do if they turned him down. "Oh, drive around Mexico until I run out of gas." He was turned down, and went to Mexico. He was my age, within a week, but always seemed younger. I think Merton saw in

John Paul not only a brother but all mankind. He had not always been kind to John Paul, brotherly rivalries being what they are. "When I think now of my childhood," Merton wrote in *The Seven Storey Mountain*, "the picture I get of my brother John Paul is this: standing in a field, about a hundred yards away from the clump of sumachs where we have built our hut, is this perplexed five-year-old kid in short pants and a kind of a leather jacket, standing quite still, with his arms hanging down at his sides, and gazing in our direction, afraid to come any nearer on account of the stones, as insulted as he is saddened, and his eyes full of indignation and sorrow. And yet he does not go away. We shout at him to get out of there, to beat it, and he does not go away. We tell him to play in some other place. He does not move.

"And there he stands, not sobbing, not crying, but angry and unhappy and offended and tremendously sad.... The law written in his nature says he must be with his elder brother, and do what he is doing: and he cannot understand why this law of love is being so wildly and unjustly violated in his case.

"Many times it was like that," Merton concludes. And that was the picture image Merton carried with him, because when John Paul arrived at Gethsemani for his farewell visit, Merton worried that John Paul would get lost in the monastery, and he did. "At that moment there flashed in my mind all the scores of times in our forgotten childhood when I had chased John Paul away with stones from the place where my friends and I were building a hut. And now, all of a sudden, here it was all over again: a situation that was externally of the same pattern: John Paul, standing confused and unhappy, at a distance which he was not able to bridge."

Then he adds: "Sometimes the same image haunts me now that he is dead, as though he were standing helpless in Purgatory, depending more or less on me to get him out of there, waiting for my prayers." The next day John Paul went off to war. "John Paul turned around and waved, and it was only then that his expression showed some possibility that he might be realizing, as I did, that we should never see each other on earth again." John Paul was sent to England; he met a girl he liked, was quickly married, and was quickly dead in an air raid against Germany. Merton wrote one of his most touching poems about John Paul's death. It goes, in part:

Sweet brother, if I do not sleep
My eyes are flowers for your tomb;
And if I cannot eat my bread,
My fasts shall live like willows where you died.
If in the heat I find no water for my thirst,
My thirst shall turn to springs for you, poor
    traveller.
Where, in what desolate and smokey country,
Lies your poor body, lost and dead?
And in what landscape of disaster
Has your unhappy spirit lost its road?

*

THE SEVEN STOREY MOUNTAIN (the title refers to Dante's ascent toward heaven) is the work that catapulted Merton into the eyes of the world. The book was written in 1944, when he was still in the first flush of monastic euphoria and disgust with the secular world. He had once remarked to his confessor that he was "tempted" to write an autobiography —the confessor laughed rather scornfully —but Dom Frederic, then the abbot, encouraged Merton, and the book was set down in what seemed like one long swoop of enthusiastic writing, with a freedom and vitality that he was unable to obtain in the biographies of saints that Dom Frederic assigned him to write during this period. Merton's agent submitted the book to Robert Giroux at Harcourt, Brace and Company, late in December 1947. Giroux accepted it immediately. The original manuscript was an immense work, which covered not only Merton's secular life in close detail—he seems to have had almost total recall for the past, though many later sections are based on his journal—but also his first years at Gethsemani.

Then came the immense job of editing

—and castrating—the manuscript. During the year before publication a large portion, perhaps as much as one third, was either seriously altered or literally thrown away on the insistence of the Trappist censors. One of them, upon his first reading, asked that the book be withheld, not on theological grounds but on the basis of its being "unripe" for publication, with the explanation that Merton was incapable of writing an auto-biography "with his present literary equipment." He was advised to take a correspondence course in English grammar. However, the abbot urged Merton to defend himself, which he did in a three-page, single-spaced typewritten letter pointing out that Harcourt Brace had thought the book worthy of publication. When it came to a confrontation over the book, it was obvious that the major objection was to its frankness, and here is where the trouble started. Merton toned down the manuscript, rewriting or omitting whatever bothered the censors, and possibly going beyond their wishes in an effort not to shock people. As far as I have been able to determine, there is not even a copy of this bowlderized material. That this material was personal and frank *is* relevant, since Merton had originally thought it worth including. The final result was that many people wondered what kind of neurotic Merton had been, to find himself such a sinner on the basis of reading Freud, Hemingway, D. H. Lawrence, some Italian pornographic novels, and a series of mild flirtations. "All that moaning and groaning over nothing," one person remarked to me. What is needed, obviously, is a careful reading between the lines. One doesn't have to prove Merton was a bad boy as a teen-ager; he says he was, and obscures the details, and that is enough.

What was left of the manuscript was still a substantial book of over four hundred pages. It was forceful enough to cause a quiet revolution among American Catholics, and then among people of many beliefs throughout the world. The first printing ran only 8000 copies; it was picked up by some small book clubs, and began to sell. It received no unusual reviews, no advertising to speak of, and no heavy promotion. Nevertheless, sales continued. By the time of Merton's ordination, the year following publication, roughly 400,000 copies of the book had been sold, and still it did not appear on the best-seller lists until the publisher complained ceaselessly over the omission. It finally ran third behind *The White Collar Zoo* and a book on canasta.

As we know, it was essentially the story of a modern intellectual from a secular, artistic, vaguely leftist background who found his way into the Church, and happiness. There are dozens of books with similar themes, yet this is the only one that touched a vital nerve in modern man. What makes it different from the others is its great evocation of a young man in an age when the soul of mankind had been laid open as never before, during world depression and unrest and the rise of both Communism and Fascism, when Europe and America seemed destined to war on a brutal and unimaginable scale. The war had ended when the book appeared, yet Merton's apocalyptic view of the world, of the suffering of Harlem and the slums, his hatred of war, was even more valid. *The Seven Storey Mountain* was more than an odyssey into the Church. It was a confrontation of the basic alienation of man with society, with the natural and supernatural forces that had nurtured him over the centuries. But most of all it was a confrontation with Christianity, basically with Merton's own vision of Catholicism. It was a great work, and it touched almost everyone who read it. It became a symbol and a guide to the plight of the contemporary world, touching Catholics and non-Catholics alike in their deep, alienated unconscious-ness. Tens of thousands of people saw themselves in Merton, felt his anguish over the black and the poor, war, the deadening effects of industrialization in its vast uprooting of humanity. If he had never written another word (and he had hoped not to), it would have been a landmark of the twentieth century. But it was, as he sensed, not an end but a beginning.

Yet *The Seven Storey Mountain* was not the only book that he was involved in during that period. While he was editing the manuscript, he had eleven other books in various stages of completion. Some of them were tremendously distasteful to him, like the biographies of various Cistercian saints he had been assigned to write; others were books he wanted to do, among them *Figures for an Apocalypse* and *The Waters of Siloe*. Not all the books appeared. Two manuscripts were lost, and another was held up for three years by the Order without explanation. During 1946 and 1947, at the height of this near-frenzied activity, he did not have a room to himself to write in. Until *The Seven Storey Mountain* made him famous, he worked under the most difficult conditions: he wrote on old sheets of paper and the backs of envelopes, and most of the writing was done in a period of four hours a week. The other monks did not know what he was working at.

The Seven Storey Mountain began to attract letters. Merton seemed to feel guilty that he had aroused people, but he was beginning to get a refreshed view of the world, which never left him and developed into an entirely new approach to reality. At the time the book appeared, he had an experience which marked him, and made him reassess his thinking. In August 1948, he was asked to accompany the Vicar General of the Trappists, who spoke French but no English, into Louisville as an interpreter. On the way to the city Merton wondered how he would face the wicked world. What happened, he wrote, was something unexpected. "I met the world and I found it no longer so wicked after all. Perhaps the things I resented about the world when I left it were defects of my own that I had

projected upon it. Now, on the contrary, everything stirred me with a deep and mute sense of compassion. . . . I seemed to have lost an eye for merely exterior detail and to have discovered, instead, a deep sense of respect and love and pity for the souls that such details never fully reveal. I went through the city, realizing for the first time in my life how good are all the people in the world and how much value they have in the sight of God." With this serious view of the world, of the kind of people he had been able to write off in his novels and in *The Seven Storey Mountain* as fools and sinners, he began to worry about what he was doing as a writer, and to be "ashamed of being famous." The fan mail he received was "a surprising and sobering experience." What seemed to have occurred to him was that he was being asked to grow up, to stop playing at monk and saint, and to *be* one.

*

AND NOW the entire focus of his life was on his ordination. "My priestly ordination was, I felt, the one great secret for which I had been born. Ten years before I was ordained, when I was in the world and seemed to be one of the men in the world most unlikely to become a priest, I had suddenly realized that for me ordination to the priesthood was, in fact, a matter of life or death, heaven or hell. As I finally came within sight of this perfect meeting with the inscrutable will of God, my vocation became clear. It was a mercy and a secret which were so purely mine that at first I intended to speak of them to no one." His ordination was something far greater than a momentary flight above the monotonous lowlands of his ordinary, everyday life. "It was a transfiguration of simple and usual things, as elevation of the plainest and most natural acts to the level of the sublime. It showed me that the charity of God was sufficient to transform earth into heaven." Ordination was a tremendously simple act, but one which was to elevate him in ways that were not to be clear until his death.

Merton (far left) and five other monks kneel
before Archbishop Joseph Floersch of Louisville
during the ordination rites.

Wearing a straw hat and the traditional Trappist robes, Merton relaxed outside the walls of Gethsemani, pleased and happy that he had attained the greatest goal of his life. On the back of his ordination card he had printed, "He walked with God and was seen no more because God took him."

Merton explains the Mass to Seymour Freedgood, saying it is a kind of ballet, with similar precise, prescribed movements and gestures. Freedgood, who had been expecting a pietistic answer to his question, looks thoughtful.

Merton enjoyed a few days outside the cloister after he was ordained. He told his friends about the reception THE SEVEN STOREY MOUNTAIN had received. Don Ameche was said to have been bidding for the movie rights (the abbot refused), hundreds of people were writing him for advice, and he was being swamped with requests from prominent priests and bishops and laymen for interviews, most of which he rejected. He did not want to be involved in the world again, he said. He found his right to privacy hard to maintain in the face of all the demands.   [facing page]

All holy souls
*   pray for us fellows,*
all Carmelites pray
all Third Orders,
all sodalities,
*   all altar societies,*
all action groups,
all inaction groups,
all beat up shut in groups,
all without money groups,
pray for the rich Trappist cheese groups
vice versa
mutual help,
*   amen, amen.*

UNPUBLISHED LITANY

AFTER ORDINATION Merton had a disheartening drying up, not only spiritually, but emotionally and creatively. "I found myself face to face with a mystery that was beginning to manifest itself in the depths of my soul and to move me with terror. Do not ask me what it was. I might apologize for it and call it 'suffering.'" His health was poor (and it seemed to get worse from then on), but what had hit him was "a sort of slow, submarine earthquake which produced strange commotions on the visible, psychological surface of my life." He talks of "abysmal testing and disintegration of my spirit," which, in December 1950, was replaced by "completely new moral resources, a spring of new life, a peace and a happiness that I had never known before and which subsisted in the face of nameless, interior terror." Eventually the peace grew, and won, and the terror subsided and became an illusion. And that was the beginning of the second Thomas Merton, the old one having been written away, having been killed and buried, with The Seven Storey Mountain. "To belong to God I have to belong to myself. I have to be alone—at least interiorly alone.... I cannot belong to people. None of me belongs to anybody but God.... No exclusiveness. Simple and free as the sky because I love everybody and am possessed by nobody, not held, not bound. In order to be not remembered or even wanted, I have to be a person that nobody knows. They can have Thomas Merton. He's dead. Father Louis—he's half dead." About the same time he told Bob Lax, "Say that Merton is dead and never existed, and is a fake. Bogus Trappist exposed. Golf trousers under the cowl. Merton wears a necktie. False priest caught giving candy to widows." He got through the crisis, and knew it, and could dispose of the past. In the middle of 1951 he wrote: "I have become very different from what I used to be. The man who began this journal [The Sign of Jonas] is dead, just as the man who finished The Seven Storey Mountain

when this journal began is also dead, and what is more, the man who was the central figure in The Seven Storey Mountain was dead over and over.... The Seven Storey Mountain is the work of a man I never even heard of."

*

ORDINATION OBVIOUSLY had not brought Merton the peace and isolation and solitude he had hoped for. Perhaps he had expected that his creative instincts would be diverted into other channels, that creative writing would now play a minor role in his life, but in his crisis he found that even writing had suddenly become almost impossible because of a certain kind of psychic impotence. But then the block was broken, and Merton the writer could not be contained. His restless, probing mind kept searching deeper and deeper. In May 1951, he was made Novice Master of a newly formed scholasticate at Gethsemani, and the work with the young monks, which demanded a heavy searching study on his own part, in the Church fathers and in Eastern Christian theology and mysticism and spirituality, led to a quickening of interest in these fields. Even then he had already renewed his interest in the Far East. In the fall of 1949 he had begun to correspond with a Hindu who had written him about Patanjali's system of yoga, and this led to numerous contacts in India, with Hindu monks and mystics. He found Patanjali hard to understand, and asked a friend of Bramachari's, named Das Gupta, for a commentary; he wrote me at this time (it was 1950) that in the end there isn't anything in Patanjali that isn't in St. John of the Cross. What was interesting was to see how it was said by a Hindu. He added the kind of remark that Catholics always make, which he was to think wrong later on when he got into Buddhism, that it seemed to him to be time for someone to baptize yoga the way St. Thomas had baptized Aristotle (and to leave the deep breathing for the people in California). Ten years later, of course, he didn't want to baptize anything. Articles, essays, books kept appearing, even though he was overburdened with routine work. His schedule was demanding. Three times a week he had a one-and-a-half hour conference with the novices, with an additional one on Sunday. Subjects would run something like the following: Monday, history of the order, the goals and the life; Tuesday or Wednesday, the Church; Friday, the liturgy; and Sunday, the Scripture of the day. Each day he had two or three meetings with individual novices, in half-hour conferences, seeing each one once a week or every second week. Then he had his preparations for classes, manual labor in the afternoons, his Mass and Office, and his own writing. Merton was in the habit of staying up at night after everyone else had gone to bed, reading and writing in his cubicle with the door closed, hoping the light wouldn't be seen. Along with this difficult schedule, he continued to have severe problems of health. There was hardly a part of his body that was not affected in one way or another, from his nose and teeth, to his chest, blood pressure, stomach and intestinal tract; he had bursitis, and was operated on for a slipped disc and for gastrointestinal ailments. The diet was difficult. From the middle of September until Easter the monastic fast was imposed. Breakfast consisted of barley coffee and two slices of bread. Lunch was leftovers from the previous day made into watery soup, potatoes and another vegetable, some fruit (often stewed rhubarb). Dinner was a cup of barley coffee, some fruit when the fast was not being observed (again it was most likely rhubarb), and cheese. But it was process cheese, as Gethsemani's own cheese was being sold; the bread was no longer the heavy Trappist black bread but a common white commercial variety. What may have been otherwise bearable was undermined by a constant state of tension between the new abbot on one side (Abbot Frederick had died in 1948) and most of the monks on the other. There were deep-rooted problems in the monastery which continued until the retirement of Abbot James shortly before Merton left for Asia. Many of the monks were affected, but Merton most of all, merely because of the fact that he was Merton. The observance of the monastic rule was felt by the monks to be literal and not in the spirit of St. Benedict; there was an unusual harshness, which was more annoying than elevating. The monastery became deeply involved in commercial transactions. Some monks thought it operated as a business and not as a religious foundation. It was expanding and founding new branches, and its cheese, fruit cake, and ham and bacon projects got to the point where everything else seemed to take a secondary role. Often the work wasn't properly organized, and monks would be given made-up work, or would be told to use machines when manual labor was more suited, both in terms of their own needs and satisfactions and suitability. A former novice said that in his opinion the monastery was a perfect example of organization life at its worst. He added that the rigid imposition of the Rule enforced an authoritarian view of power that had nothing to do with the development of personality. Over and over again the understanding of the Rule was contradicted. It was hard to put up with contradictions after learning about the true monastic life. The letter of the Rule was killing, and the large number of applicants and the high rate of their subsequent leaving shows the dichotomy: men were attracted by what Merton saw in monasticism and what he wrote about it, and turned away by the life as it was dictated by the abbot. It was a trial for the young novices: it was even more so for Merton. However, he rarely mentioned his own problems, and he was extremely careful not to disillusion the novices. He left a man to work his way through the situation, trying not to shake anyone up. But if a novice began to express his doubts and hesitations and problems, then Merton would encourage him to talk freely

and openly. Many novices left sooner or later, and leaving was a constant temptation for Merton himself, much as he tried to pretend it was not. Before his ordination he had talked to his confessor about joining the Carthusians; he had wanted to be a hermit, and the interest in the charterhouse never left. There were always rumors that he had left—some obviously based on his known chafing under the abbot, but others came from the phenomenon of the Merton impostors, the tramps who presented themselves at rectory and convent doors asking for help and claiming to be Merton and just out of Gethsemani. In 1953, Merton actively petitioned to be transferred to the Carthusians; this request was turned down by the Prefect of Religions and by Rome, but that did not end his restlessness. Sometimes he entertained the idea of going to Mount Athos and being a hermit among the colonies of Greek and Russian Orthodox monks; in the middle of the 1960s he was invited to join a new Benedictine foundation in Central America. This was a real temptation, which he considered at length. I think he was allowed to have his hermitage (it was ready for use in January 1961), primarily to keep him at Gethsemani.

Meanwhile the struggles continued: on one level, all the daily problems of health and bad food and the irrational application of the Rule and the extra

Now a priest, Merton felt he had reached the summit of his life. But almost immediately he began to experience a spiritual and intellectual drying up. He experienced months of depression and inability to put down his thoughts. He had taken the vow of stability as a kind of guarantee against the life of wandering he had experienced as a child and a teen-ager, but now he began to feel a kind of physical restriction, which he eventually solved with a renewed inner search. He was led into studies not only of the standard Christian saints, but the Desert Fathers, and then to holy men of other cultures and religions. He began to correspond again with Bramachari.

work, and underneath, the widening, deepening, truly mystical search into the interior reaches of the soul that was expressed in his writings. Every step was attained with suffering and loneliness (as opposed to the *solitude* he was seeking) and anguish. His writings during this period were entirely "Christian," in fact, Catholic in the specific sense, and I doubt that he published anything that did not have an imprimatur and bear an immediate application to the life of the Church. But the journal he began to keep, starting in 1956 (it was published ten years later under the title of *Conjectures of a Guilty Bystander*), showed other currents running into his life. He was reading Karl Barth, St. John Perse, and a large number of Latin-American poets (in both Spanish and Portuguese; many of them he later translated), and in particular Gandhi and books about Gandhi. He began to reflect more on truth, violence, war and the Christian's commitment, technology and the industrial man; his reading and writing ranged further and further away from traditional monastic subjects. He became interested in the Muslim sufis, and in Chinese philosophy.

His thinking suddenly was given a sharp turn, when in the spring of 1959 he sent a copy of his book on the Desert Fathers to Dr. D. T. Suzuki, a leading Zen Buddhist scholar, with the suggestion that perhaps they had something in common with the Japanese Zen masters. This led to an exchange of letters and the eventual publication of points of view by both Merton and Suzuki. Nearly eight years later Merton stated that he thought some of his remarks in this dialogue were "confusing," and that they are an example of how not to approach Zen. But he had taken the turn: His life was now to be focused on Buddhism and peace, and there was little he wrote that was not connected, even vaguely, with one or the other. Out of his deep acceptance of Christianity, he was now trying to transcend nation and culture and time, and make himself—and mankind—relevant in the light of eternity. This meant giving up parochial identifications, and taking the Church not only symbolically but literally when she talked about peace, as he was expected to do when she preached Christ. There comes a point where the bottom drops out of the world of factuality and of the ordinary. He was trying to push the contradictions of life to the limit. The last section of *Conjectures of a Guilty Bystander* is headed "The Madman Runs to the East." He took it from a Zen proverb:

> The madman runs to the East
> and his keeper runs to the East:
> Both are running to the East,
> Their purposes differ.

Day in and day out, Merton thought, wrote, preached peace and the East. I think that a lot of his readers, particularly the very devout ones from stanch Catholic backgrounds, began to drop out. I find this resistance marked even now, when I talk to friends who appreciated *The Seven Storey Mountain* and the later "religious" writings, but have an uneasy suspicion that Merton had flipped on the subjects of peace and the East and was being "heretical." But the fact is, what was to come in the 1960s was not an aberration but the entire point of his life as a layman and especially as a Trappist. The trip was inevitable, inexorable, and it was independent of rules, regulations, bad health, monastic discipline, constant tensions and the very severe attempts of the Trappist censors to silence him.

*

IF HE couldn't become a Carthusian, he could at least be a Trappist hermit. The Benedictine Rule allows monks to work toward the eremitical life—in fact, it is a recognized goal, though most monks remained cenobites—and from time to time there had been hermits at Gethsemani. It had been on Merton's mind for many years, and it was a subject he constantly brought up before the abbot. Eventually he got the hermitage,

but he was forced to trickery and pressure and evasion to obtain it. It annoyed him that he had to act so, and that he could not get it openly and directly as should have been possible. After a long period, the abbot finally gave him permission for a hermitage. "Father Abbot thought I was going to build a little wooden hut to sit and think in," Merton told me in discussing the development of the hermitage, "but I had the novices build a real cement-block house." It was a large building—better than most of the houses the local farmers and workers in the area, which are often nothing more than rural slums—with a large living room and several smaller rooms. However, the abbot had his revenge: he was terribly annoyed when he first saw the hermitage, and Merton was not allowed to complete it. Merton did not get a toilet or kitchen or chapel until the year before he was to go to Asia. Meanwhile, it was heated only by the fireplace, which hardly warmed more than a small area, leaving the rest of the living room, which was where he studied, worked and prayed, bitterly cold (temperatures in Kentucky can often drop to near zero); and his toilet was the open woods, in snow or rain or Kentucky mist. He heated coffee at the fireplace, but most of his meals were cold scraps of food (chunks of ham or sardines) which he brought up from the monastery. He was suffering terribly from stomach trouble and diarrhea, but apparently no real care was taken about his diet, except that he was told not to eat milk and cheese and other dairy products. After a visit to him one winter, I told some mutual friends about his living conditions, which I thought were appalling for a sick man (and even for a man in normal health), and wanted to write to the Abbot, but the strong advice from people who knew both Merton and Abbot James was that it would be a mistake to interfere, and that nothing could be accomplished. Now, several years later, I am still not sure what should have been done. One person sided with the Abbot and said that "Merton was always complaining." I think he had something to complain about. He was expected to write, which he did, and to work and pray, which he also did, but he was expected to do so under appallingly difficult conditions. A New York friend of Merton's said after his death that in his opinion the Abbot had it in for Tom.

But even with the difficulties the hermitage was necessary. It had a beautiful, sweeping view of a valley, and it was set amid a grove of young trees. It was isolated from the monastery, and not many of the monks bothered Merton. "These novices never learned how to walk," said Merton, "and the jeep won't go through the trees. So I've got peace." But daily he went to the monastery to say Mass, until he got permission for the chapel (that was in 1967), and for whatever meetings and conferences were necessary. He attended the monastic Office less and less, and spent more and more time in meditation and study. He had always had a rigorous schedule for work: he normally arose at two, had some coffee, and began to work. He had the early hours of the morning to himself, and by the time the outside world was beginning its own workday, he had already done a full day's work. And he still had the daylight hours for further work, study, prayer and monastic duties. This schedule explains the sheer velocity of Merton's work, the flowing productivity. He was tremendously well organized and logical; all was done neatly and quickly; he kept carbons of letters and articles, and everything was filed properly. Beyond that, he had a fantastic ability to read and comprehend everything, to filter ideas and thoughts through his incredible mind, to sort out the irrelevant and to focus on the essentials. He had the habit of doing a draft of an article (which many writers would have considered a finished work) and having it mimeographed by one of the other monks. This draft might be sent to a few friends for comments; often there would be a second version, and even a third. Meanwhile the censors were going over the material. These mimeographed versions of articles sometimes resulted in an article, in either identical or alternate forms, being printed simultaneously by different magazines. His volume of correspondence was such that even with his filing system and his memory he could not always recall to whom he had sent material. But most often there were few such mistakes. I don't think he ever charged a smaller magazine for his work, but the larger ones (such as *Life*) paid the usual rates. Eventually, articles were collected in the proper categories and published in books. At the time of his departure he left behind outlines of five or six books to be made out of recently published material.

*

HE RETURNED over and over again, once he had found his new direction in the 1960s, to these basic themes: war and peace, violence and nonviolence, and Buddhism. He began to run into opposition from the Trappist censors on a scale never before encountered. They stopped a very innocuous article on Pierre Teilhard de Chardin at a time when every Catholic publication was writing about him, and they constantly held up or castrated articles on peace, as if a monk had no business writing about peace. A high superior told Merton, "It is not your place to write about nuclear war: that is for the bishops." Then a moral theologian told him, "How can you expect the bishops to commit themselves on the question of peace and war, unless they are advised by their theologians?" When he addressed an open letter to the American hierarchy on peace and war in 1965 it was ignored. Later he wrote to his own bishop in Louisville in a very warm yet demanding letter to ask for a firm, Christian statement on the same subject, and never received a reply. He was forced to publish a book of essays by different contributors anonymously, with himself listed merely as another contributor and not as editor because of this hostility on the part of superiors. A book called *Peace*

71

Merton stands on the porch of his hermitage. It was ready for use in January 1961, though it lacked heat, a toilet and a kitchen. Winters were hard for him, especially when the temperature dropped close to zero. He did not get the necessary facilities or improvements or a personal chapel until shortly before he left for Asia.

Merton tries to keep warm in 15° weather. In order to have time and quiet for meditation and work, he paid a terrible price by not having the minimal facilities. However, he still had the peace and seclusion he was seeking.

in the Post-Christian Era, which states in the clearest, most Catholic, moral, unambiguous and responsible terms the role of the Christian in a nuclear age, was stopped dead by the censors. Another book, a collection of essays on peace, was also stopped though some of the material had already appeared in censored form. The ex-novice I have quoted earlier remarked that "it is fantastic, to think that a monk is not allowed to write about peace." He added, "the other monks in Gethsemani never knew what Merton had said about peace; they were not allowed to read whatever he did get published." Consequently, Merton was involved in a kind of guerrilla warfare for peace. He circulated articles privately though extensively; some pieces were published, though often with emendations, so that what he was thinking was clear. He committed himself completely to the peace movement; he lent his name to several organizations, though he wasn't always happy about the haphazard manner in which it was used, or the way in which the movement sometimes operated. And what seems clear now, is that he was the only well-known Catholic in America to take an open stand. All the other Catholics in the movement, with the exception of Dorothy Day, were known only within their own circle. It was a heroic stance, and in the light of his entire commitment, the only one he could have taken. Of course it's true that nothing could be done against him: he could not be sent any further away, be any more isolated; the food couldn't be any worse, he had no car to lose. There was always the question of "prudence." He was completely "prudent" in the eschatological sense, completely imprudent in terms of ordinary day-to-day Catholic living. So, he chose his soul over prudence.

In the article on Pierre Teilhard de Chardin, which was banned by the Trappist censors, he wrote, in summary of an idea of Teilhard's, but one which was essentially his as well, "One of the most formal obligations of the Christian is to struggle against evil, whether it be moral or physical. The Christian can only resign himself passively to the acceptance of evil when it is quite clear that he is powerless to do anything about it. Hence it is an utterly false Christianity which preaches the supine acceptance of social injustice, ignorance, impossible working conditions, and war as though it were virtue to 'take' all this and 'offer it up' without even attempting to change anything. His view of Christian virtue is far from the stoic resignation which accepts the decrees of 'fate' with a carefully cultivated insensibility. He has no patience with a concept of 'purity of intention' which is completely divorced from the act to be performed. How can we have a really 'pure' intention to do the will of God if, in fact, we are completely indifferent to the quality of the work performed in response to the demands of life which are in fact God's own demand?

"The genuine 'purity' of Christian action will, indeed, teach man to work without undue concern for the results of his efforts, but will not make him utterly indifferent to the work itself since he will see clearly that his work is a communion with God, His creator, in which he not only unites himself to God but also 'saves' and transforms the material world 'in Christ.'"

*

HIS FEELINGS on war were clear from the beginning. Merton registered for the draft as a conscientious objector, but was classified 1-B because of his teeth, this being a temporary deferment. But even before there had been a draft, he wrote in his journal: "If we go to war, it will be first of all to defend our investments, our business, our money. In certain terms it may be useful to defend all these things, and expedient to protect our business so that everybody may have jobs, but if anybody holds up American business as a shining example of justice, or American politics as a shining example of honesty and purity that is really quite a joke.

"And if this is a joke, it is also a bit blasphemous to get up and say that just because Germany started the actual fighting, ultimately Germany is to blame for everything, and God is on the side of England and the democracies and all the enemies of Germany.

"To try to make God the defender of any one side in this war is simply to reduce Him to the level of a Nazi, and no greater blasphemy is possible. But, besides that, it is irrational to the point of lunacy. We know the Nazis half expect, from moment to moment, to be struck down by fire from heaven, because they have an eradicable suspicion that there is a God somewhere, and if there is one, He must be a Nazi, and ready to destroy even His friends at the first sign of anything that displeases Him."

Later he wrote: "If we are ever going to have peace again, we will have to hate war for some better reason than that we fear to lose our houses, our refrigerators, our cars, our legs, our lives. If we are ever to get peace, we have got to desire something more than reefers [pot] and anesthetics. That is all we seem to want: anything to avoid pain."

After the summer in Olean in 1940, he saw a German propaganda film in New York, which upset him. He remarked that, "It is no joke that the world is going to turn into something infinitely repulsive and horrible when it is remade in the image of people who believe in this kind of thing; and the tragedy of it is, if we fight Hitler, we will become like him, too, we will turn into something just as dirty as he is. If we are going to beat him, we will have to." This idea seemed to be ever on his mind. On another occasion he wrote that, "A people that loves peace only because war is horrible, degrading, unprofitable and extremely filthy and revolting is very likely to get mixed up in a war quite soon, and also, to get beaten in it. No matter how horrible anything is that we can bring about by our own wills, there has to be some better reason for avoiding it than merely that it is physically 'horrible.'" He had no illusions about Hitler, however:

"Slavery is exactly what he plans, for as many as he can actually enslave. The others will be dominated by starvation or, at least, a relentless economic and military pressure." He does not think Roosevelt and Churchill can imagine what an Allied victory will mean. "If they are going to police the world, it means keeping on foot a colossal Army and Navy for years, and it means being able to sit on the world the way Hitler intends to sit on it. Obviously there is only one Hitler now, and if we become as bad as he is later (which doesn't look probable), there is not much advantage for the world at large, in our winning this war." His fear was that "The present capitalist system has got certain terrific weaknesses which, if it survives the war at all, which it may, will make inevitable a series of revolutions that will be almost as bad as a German victory: and that is clearly not something to die for! Especially since one of the results of these revolutions may be an 'order' something like Nazism or Fascism or the Dictatorship of the Proletariat, but most likely Fascism, in this country." I don't think he ever solved the dilemma his reasoning had posed, between not opposing Hitler and letting him destroy the world on one hand, and fighting to a final victory and assuming the characteristics of the Nazis. Merton continued to oppose World War II, but his greatest vehemence, his anger and skill as a polemicist (and this along with his denunciations of the systems that led to poverty and misery in the world) went to his attacks on the war in Vietnam and the factors behind it. It was a constant campaign with him, and not even his bishops and the American hierarchy were spared his attention. Outsiders were often puzzled that a cloistered monk with the vow of silence should, first of all, have such thorough knowledge of the war, and secondly that he should write at such length, and unceasingly, about the war and its horrors, and the fact that having proclaimed ourselves as the most moral nation in the world, we were at the same time being the

From his porch Merton had a long sweeping view of the rolling countryside. His companions were squirrels and chipmunks and birds, and an occasional Kentucky farmer who would drop by to chat.

most immoral. I once showed him a photograph I had taken in Vietnam of a young mother and child who were burned by napalm dropped by an American plane. He looked at it a long time, wondering not only about the tragic burns on the two victims, but what had happened to the interior sensibilities of the young American men who could drop such a weapon without an apparent thought of the consequences.

In Olean he used to go for long walks in the woods, or just sit quietly by the cottage when everyone else had gone off on other projects. He wrote that last summer: "Here it is very quiet and sunny. In front of me there is a bush covered with pale white blossoms that do not smell of anything much. Somewhere under some thorns and weeds a cricket sings drily. Everything is quiet and sunny and good. . . . It is possible to imagine a man coming silently out of these woods into the open grass space before me and aiming a gun and shooting me dead in this chair, and going away. Even though it is sunlight, the woods might well fill, all at once, with the clack and roar of tanks. The aeroplane that went by an hour ago might have been filled with bombs, but it just wasn't. There is nothing too fantastic to believe any more, because everything is fantastic. There is no fighting here now, but there could very well be plenty tomorrow."

*

MERTON'S APPEAL touched many people who were not Catholic. Joan Baez came to see him at Gethsemani, in December 1965, accompanied by Ira Sandperl, who ran a peace center with her. Lenny Bruce often ended his nightclub act by reading Merton's chilling "A Devout Meditation in Memory of Adolph Eichmann," in a German accent. Merton begins by saying that "One of the most disturbing facts that came out in the Eichmann trial was that a psychiatrist examined him and pronounced him *perfectly sane*. I do not doubt it at all, and that is why I find it disturbing." He continues: "The sanity of Eichmann is disturbing. We equate sanity with a sense of justice, with humaneness, with prudence, with the capacity to love and understand other people. We rely on the sane people of the world to preserve it from barbarism, madness, destruction. And it now begins to dawn on us that it is precisely the *sane* ones who are the most dangerous.

"It is the sane ones, the well-adapted ones, who can without qualms and without nausea aim the missiles and press the buttons that will initiate the great festival of destruction that they, *the sane ones*, have prepared." He points out that there will be no danger from psychotics, as the sane ones will keep them from the buttons. "No one suspects the sane, and the sane ones will have *perfectly good reasons*, logical, well-adjusted reasons, for firing the shot. They will be obeying sane orders that have come sanely down the chain of command. And because of their sanity they will have no qualms at all. When the missiles take off, then, *it will be no mistake*." He makes the distressing point that Christians want to be sane like everybody else. They can become sane like Eichmann. "Eichmann was sane. The generals and fighters on both sides, in World War II, the ones who carried out the total destruction of entire cities, these were the sane ones. Those who have invented and developed atomic bombs, thermonuclear bombs, missiles; who have planned the strategy of the next war; who have evaluated the various possibilities of using bacterial and chemical agents: these are not the crazy people, they are the sane people. The ones who cooly estimate how many millions of victims can be considered expendable in a nuclear war, I presume they do all right with the Rorschach ink blots too. On the other hand, you will probably find that the pacifists and the ban-the-bomb people are, quite seriously, just as we read in *Time*, a little crazy." His matter-of-fact account of the bombing of Hiroshima, *Original Child Bomb* ("Original Child" was the Japanese term for the bomb) has been a favorite on-the-air reading for

WBAI and other underground FM radio stations. The book which was held up for an unconscionably long time by the Trappist censors, who apparently wanted it banned altogether, is subtitled "Points for meditation to be scratched on the walls of a cave." It simply recounts in forty-one numbered paragraphs the dropping of the first atomic bomb on Hiroshima. The code names, Little Boy, Trinity, the Papacy, give an added dimension of horror in Merton's narrative, as he points out that the Japanese had already been trying to negotiate for peace through the Russians and that a group of sixty American scientists had petitioned the President not to drop the bomb without a convincing warning and an opportunity for the Japanese to surrender. "As to the Original Child that was now born," Merton writes, "President Truman summed up the philosophy of the situation in a few words. 'We found the bomb,' he said, 'and we used it.' Since that summer many other bombs have been 'found.' What is going to happen? At the time of writing [1962], after a season of brisk speculation, men seem to be fatigued by the whole question."

*

THE PEACE of mankind was one concern, the peace of the human soul was another. The latter took the form of a study of oriental monasticism that went beyond mere curiosity or scholarly pursuits. As a Trappist, Merton sought solitude, meditation and aloneness with God. He searched for the interior peace that every man should have in order to be a functioning, integrated, normal individual. Merton was searching not for a religion—which he had—but a discipline of a different color and intensity from the Trappists'. He turned to Zen Buddhism. To Merton, Zen was not the slippery, one-upmanship game that Zen became for many Westerners, but a mature, demanding, responsible and rock-hard discipline that was the antithesis of Western thinking, which, he believed, had become too stratified, too codified

and "logical" to the exclusion of true thought.

One of the Eastern philosophers who interested him—to give a single example from Merton's many studies—was a Chinese sage named Chuang Tzu who lived in the fourth and third centuries before Christ. Chuang Tzu is considered a forerunner of the Zen movement, as it later developed in China and Japan. Merton spent some five or six years in meditating upon the works of Chuang Tzu, and annotating them, finally producing a book of "translations," which are a combination of poetic rephrasing of true translations by other authors and his own special insights into the master's mind. "I have been a Christian monk for 25 years," Merton wrote about his "translations" of the Chuang Tzu sayings and parables, "and inevitably one comes in time to see life from a viewpoint that has been common to all solitaries and recluses of all ages and all cultures.... The philosophical temper of Chuang Tzu is, I believe, profoundly original and sane. It can, of course, be misunderstood. But it is basically simple and direct. It seeks, as does all the greatest philosophical thought, to go immediately to the heart of things." Then he himself goes directly to the heart of Chuang Tzu. "Chuang Tzu is not concerned with words and formulas about reality, but with the direct existential grasp of reality in itself. Such a grasp is necessarily obscure and does not lend itself to abstract analysis. It can be presented in a parable, a fable, or a funny story about a conversation between two philosophers. ... The 'way' of Chuang Tzu is mysterious because it is so simple that it can get along without being a way at all. Least of all is it a 'way out.' Chuang Tzu would have agreed upon this kind of way when you leave all ways and, in some sense, get lost."

Merton's studies of Buddhism had gone far beyond Chuang Tzu when he died. His essays—and those published were already considerable—were only the beginning of what had promised to be years of work and meditation on the massive body of Eastern thought and philosophy. Merton saw Buddhism not in the limited, passive terms which brings its dismissal by Western philosophers (and this has been one of the faults of Catholics particularly) but as a dynamic and creative force which had been the way for millions of people for longer than Christianity had existed. He did not try to "baptize" Buddhism as the average Christian might. He was not interested in picking odds and ends from the East and amalgamating them into Christianity. Buddhism had its own very valid and true existence, and he was trying to shed the restrictions of the Western mind in reaching out for it. He went through tremendous growing pains in each step of his life and each meant a major upheaval. His study of the East was such an experience.

I WILL continue briefly with some remarks about Merton's study of Zen. He makes the point (in Zen and the Birds of Appetite) that Zen and Christianity, as structures, as systems, and as religions, are utterly alien to one another. The matter is very complex, and Westerners immediately preclude all possibility of understanding Zen by trying to get it defined, in Western terms. Merton says, "Zen is consciousness unstructured by particular form or particular system, a trans-cultural, trans-religious, trans-formed consciousness. . . . In Zen enlightenment, the discovery of the 'original face before you were born' is the discovery not that one sees Buddha but that one is Buddha and that Buddha is not what the images in the temple led one to expect: for there is no longer any image, and consequently nothing to see, no one to see it, and a Void in which no image is even conceivable. 'The true seeing,' said Shen Hui, 'is when there is no seeing.'" Merton repeats: "What this means then is that Zen is outside all structures and forms." Later he says, "The way to see it is not first to define Zen and then apply

In the hermitage, Merton began to take long, quiet looks at the world. He remarked that as time goes on one comes to look upon the world in general and the Church in particular with a kind of indifference that would shock many. He said that there was every reason why the life of the Catholic Kirk (as he phrased it) should induce all forms of neurosis and anxiety and everything else right up the line. The way the Christian faith is lived, he said, is so schizophrenic that it is a wonder one can be at the same time a Christian and sane, that is, a Christian according to the approved patterns and forms. He said bluntly that the present institutional structure of the Church is often in practice "unjust, unhuman, arbitrary and even absurd in its functioning." He had been running through a lot of private difficulties. He remarked offhandedly to someone: "I'm in jail and sitting on the faggots while the head Inquisitor fumbles with the matchbox which is luckily in his other pair of trousers." He wrote in his journal that he wished "the religious life were less of a perpetual cold war . . . between subjects and superiors." At one point he said he was "ascending the mountain of love on all fours and I don't know where the hell to look next." He talked about "just the depression of living under constant absurd attrition." But added: "Fortunately I have the woods."

In the 1950s Merton took up drawing again. He began to work in an oriental, calligraphic style which was part derivation from Chinese ideograms, part symbols of buildings and landscapes.

85

the definition.... The real way to study Zen is to penetrate the outer shell and taste the inner kernel which cannot be defined. Then one realizes in oneself the reality which is being talked about." In the light of what happened to Merton in his meeting with the Tibetan monks in India, and their reception of him, it is obvious—to me (and I cannot document it, of course)—that they accepted him as one who has passed beyond ordinary experience, that is, Merton apparently had already had, at least once and if not frequently, "direct and pure experience on a metaphysical level, liberated from verbal formulas and linguistic conceptions." The interior evidence, the "feel" of his later writings on Zen indicate this, without its being said in so many words. I think he had already reached the point where words were superfluous; his letter from New Delhi on November 9th to Gethsemani is marked by its flatness; it is essentially a "duty" letter, and what he had experienced, and was to experience, could not be verbalized. Hence the pedantic accounting of traffic and food and minor events.

*

AND THEN there was the question of Merton's racial attitudes, which are clear and to the point. His identification with brown, yellow, red and black was complete. As early as 1931 (he was only sixteen then, and without any of the influences that move today's sensitive young people), he argued with the football captain at Oakham about Gandhi, who, Merton insisted, was right and that India was, in demanding that the British withdraw, and that the millions of people of India had a perfect right to run their own country. "How could Gandhi be right when he was *odd?* And how could I be right if I was on the side of someone who had the wrong kind of skin, and left altogether too much of it exposed?" His belief in the rights of those who were not white to their own lives, land and culture and civilization never changed: it became more and more

adamant, no matter how it was expressed. The dichotomy between the races was always there. In a poem about Cuba he wrote:

> The white girls lift their heads like trees,
> The black girls go
> Reflected like flamingoes in the street.
>
> The white girls sing as shrill as water,
> The black girls talk as quiet as clay.

Later he wrote Lax: "I am trying to figure out some way I can get nationalized as a Negro as I am tired of belonging to the humiliating white race. One wants at times the comfort of belonging to a race that one can like and respect. This unfortunately seems to be something that has been concluded beforehand for everyone." Less than two weeks later he wrote again: "What I said about the human race was serious and I am glad you took it serious. I am going to write to the Govt. about resigning from the human race. Or at least the white part, which is not by all accounts the most human." He said quite the same, in different terms, to James Baldwin, in discussing the inability of whites to have even the slightest comprehension of what blacks are and what they want. In his beautiful, compassionate and moving "Letters to a White Liberal," which should be read carefully in its entirety, he made the point that "The actions and attitudes of white Christians all, without exception, contain a basic and axiomatic assumption of white superiority, even when the pleas of the Negro for equal rights are hailed with the greatest benevolence. It is simply taken for granted that, since the white man is superior, the *Negro wants to become a white man.* And we, liberals and Christians that we are, advance generally, with open arms, to embrace our little black brother and welcome him into white society.

"The Negro not only is not grateful, he is not even impressed. In fact, he shows by his attitude that he is at the same time antagonized and disgusted by our stupidity." Then he makes the very important statement that "For some unknown reason, the white man (especially the Southern white) does not seem to realize that he has been rather closely observed, for the last two centuries, by his Negro slaves, servants, share-croppers, concubines, and bastards. He does not seem to be aware that they know a great deal about him, and, in fact, understand him in some ways better than he understands himself." In talking specifically of Catholic attitudes toward the Negro, he says: "When the Catholic Church gives the impression that it regards the South as a vast potential pool of 'Negro converts' in which a zealous and ardent white apostolate can transform a few million Uncle Toms into reasonably respectable imitations of white Catholics, this actually does very little to make the Negro respect the truth of Christ, practically nothing to help him understand the mystery of Christ." He concludes on a prophetic note: "By and large, in the midst of the clamor of every possible kind of jaded and laughable false prophets, the voice of the American Negro has in it a genuine prophetic ring. Who knows if we will ever get another chance to hear it?" He warns that if the white man does not respond, the awakened Negro will forget his moment of Christian hope and Christian inspiration. "He will no longer be the gentle, wide-eyed child singing hymns while the police dogs lunge at his throat. There will be no more hymns and no more prayer vigils. He will become a Samson whose African strength flows back into his arms. He will suddenly pull the pillars of white society crashing down upon himself and his oppressor. And perhaps, somewhere out of the ruins, a new world (a black world) will one day rise."

But Merton's disillusionment with his own people, with Christians and pointedly with Catholics, is evident in the final paragraphs. "This is the 'message' which the Negro is trying to give white America. I have spelled it out for myself, subject to correction, in order to see whether a white man is even capable of grasping the words, let alone believing them. For the rest, you have Moses and and the Prophets: Martin Luther King, James Baldwin and the others. Read them, and see for yourself what they are saying."

Eldridge Cleaver was particularly touched by Merton, and felt him alternately confused, transpired and "some kind of nut." Cleaver first heard about Merton in San Quentin, and he felt that Merton's monastery was very much like a prison. "My secret disgust was that in many ways I was nothing but a monk, and how I loathed that view of myself!" Cleaver was transferred to Folsom Prison for being an agitator and put into solitary confinement. However, he was allowed to read, and one of the books available to him was *The Seven Storey Mountain*.

"I was tortured by that book because Merton's suffering, in his quest for God, seemed all in vain to me. At the time, I was a Black Muslim chained in the bottom of a pit by the Devil. Did I expect Allah to tear down the walls and set me free? To me, the language and the symbols of religion were nothing but weapons of war. I had no other purpose for them. All the gods are dead except the god of war. I wished that Merton had stated in secular terms the reasons he withdrew from the political, economic, military, and social system into which he was born, seeking refuge in a monastery.

"Despite my rejection of Merton's theistic world view, I could not keep him out of the room. He shouldered his way through the door. Welcome, Brother Merton. I give him a bear hug. Most impressive to me was Merton's description of New York's black ghetto— Harlem. I liked it so much I copied out the heart of it in longhand. Later, after getting out of solitary, I used to keep this passage in mind when delivering Black Muslim lectures to other prisoners." The passage that struck Cleaver is this:

"Here in this huge dark, steaming slum, hundreds of thousands of Negroes are herded together like cattle, most of them with nothing to eat and nothing to do. All the senses and imagination and sensibilities and emotions and sorrows and desires and hopes and ideas of a race with vivid feelings and deep emotional reactions are forced in upon themselves, bound inward by an iron ring of frustration: the predjudice that hems them in with its four insurmountable walls. In this huge cauldron, estimable natural gifts, wisdom, live music, science, poetry are stamped down and left to boil with the dregs of an elementary corrupted nature, and thousands upon thousands of souls are destroyed by vice and misery and degradation, obliterated, wiped out, washed from the register of the living, dehumanized.

"What has not been devoured, in your dark furnace, Harlem, by marijuana, by gin, by insanity, hysteria, syphilis?"

Cleaver then says: "For a while, whenever I felt myself softening, relaxing, I had only to read that passage to become once more a rigid flame of indignation. It had precisely the same effect on me that Elijah Muhammad's writings used to have, or the words of Malcolm X, or the words of any spokesman of the oppressed in any land. I vibrate sympathetically to any protest against tyranny."

*

IN AN ESSAY called "Cargo Theology," on the Cargo cults of the South Pacific, Merton tackles the question of race, of white, brown and black at length. By way of explanation, the Cargo cults (the most famous of which are based in New Guinea) are messianic, eschatological, cosmic movements in which the adherents believe that the white man has a special means of communicating with God, and that if the native learns this special secret, he too will be able to share in these blessings. What happened—to condense a very complex movement—was

Merton, as he looked at the height of his powers. He was deep in his Buddhist studies, and the monastery had become a background for his work rather than the subject. Less than three years later he was dead.

Standing atop a knoll outside the monastery Merton calls down the wrath of God upon warmongers and racists before a statue of St. Joseph.

On a cold winter's day Merton looks tired and drawn. He liked to stroll through the vast acres of the abbey. One of his favorite haunts was a pond which he visited when he wanted to get away from the monastery and think out his work. He had a small quarterly magazine called MONK'S POND, which was inspired by his walks.

The rigors of years of primitive accommodations without proper heat began to take their toll on Merton. Though bundled up against the cold, his face shows that "winter" look. When he entered Gethsemani in 1941 the monastery was not heated, the monks changed their robes only twice a year, their work clothes were washed but once a month, and they had to get permission to bathe. Although Abbot James changed many of the harsher regulations, Merton's first years in the hermitage were also passed without ordinary facilities.

that the natives realized that a white man needed only to send a message, a piece of paper, in order to receive a ship or a plane load in return, with food, equipment, medicines. These movements reached their peak after World War II, after the Americans and Australians had left the jungle islands of the South Pacific. Some natives even built decoy airplanes out of bamboo to lure the jets passing high overhead to the now abandoned air strips left over from the war.

Merton takes the Cargo movement as the basis for a discussion of the relationship between the white man and the remainder of the world, essentially the undeveloped, poor world. Drawing upon three excellent books on the subject of Cargo, he says that every man, no matter what color, operates on a "substrata of mythdream which underlies all human activities. This mythdream" [and here he is quoting a scholar named Kenelm Burridge] "is a body of notions derived from a variety of sources, such as rumors, personal experiences, desires, conflicts, and ideas about the total environment which find expressions in mythdreams, popular stories and anecdotes." He says first—to the white man—that "Cargo is a pagan superstition which has to replaced by an enlightened Christian and progressive view of life. That is [the] *Western* view of life." But, he adds (and emphasizes) "we delude ourselves that we are utterly scientific, that we have no myths. But that is one of our chief myths.... Our mythdream assures us that we are totally objective, scientific people. But we live embedded in an enormous amount of mythology."

He adds parenthetically "that the solitary life is, among other things, a life of critical withdrawal from the general mythdream. I am a critic of the American mythdream and open to other mythdreams. This is why I'm interested in Cargo: because I can see the Cargo mythdream too and to some extent participate in it and criticize the American

mythdream in terms of the New Guinea mythdream. This is, I would say, for me part of my personal vocation. It is part of my 'contemplative life.'

"In other words, it is important not to escape from all the mythdreams into a realm of pure logic but, on the contrary, to be able to move from one mythdream into another and at the same time *to be aware of a transcendent common mythdream which is basic to the entire human race.*"

Merton analyzes the attempts of the Kanakas (the natives of New Guinea) and others to make Cargo successful. I won't retrace the details, but the message, he says, boils down to this: "That men are brothers and that some men have been separated from others by the fact of having greater gifts and greater skill, but that this does not mean that they are essentially better.... The fact that some men are more fortunate than others does not mean they are superior, still less that they are not brothers of the others."

But, in any case, in the myth of Cargo, "the native is grappling with the idea of his 'inferiority' and with a sense of guilt which has been instilled into him by the superior endowment and prosperity of the white man. In so doing, he is arriving at a basic truth. He is trying to tell himself, 'look, you do not have to feel guilty because you're black. It does not mean that you are worse. You do not have to feel guilty because the white man has Cargo and you don't. This is not a sign that you are bad. It's not a sign that you are helpless. You can and should have Cargo too.'"

He then puts Cargo into wider terms: "Black people everywhere are in a tremendous identity crisis, struggling with something which we whites do not realize, struggling with a feeling of guilt because they are black and trying to arrive at a conviction that being black does not mean being worse.

"In Black Power, as in Cargo, the Negro is seeking to establish first of all his identity as one capable of getting equality for and by himself, rather than waiting to receive it as a benevolent gift on the white man's terms."

What is important for the white man, for "us," he says, is to learn to read into these movements what is really there and thus deliver ourselves from the awful white superstition of utter and absolute superiority. "The superstition that we have the only answer and, of course, we're willing to help black brother, but the help that we offer to our little black brother is offered in such arrogant, vain, self-complacent terms that it means that we will not help him to be anything until he can be exactly like us and we make it impossible for him to be exactly like us. So we put him in an impossible bind and then wonder why he feels so anguished."

The native myth, he says, reflects "an entirely different concept of rights. It is at odds with our more pragmatic concept. Our view is that you have a right to what you're smart enough to acquire. Their concept is that you have a right to the necessities of life *because you are a human being.* All human beings have a right to the same advantages, to the same opportunities."

"Our mythdream is a racist mythdream. The white man is fundamentally a racist. White European, White Anglo-Saxon, Protestant and Catholic too: we are all living in a mythdream which is essentially racist and we do not realize it. Endemic racism is part of our dream of ourselves and our estimate of ourselves. Even when we think we are being nice and fair and just and so forth, we are living and acting by a dream that makes fairness and justice impossible. Even when we are being kind and liberal our kindness and liberality are tinged with unconscious racism. And Black Power, among other things, is trying to tell us."

[On another occasion, in 1963, he remarked that "The Black Muslims, with hard shiny heads, with frowns, with muscles, drilling for self-defense (and not nonviolent either), have ceased to look upon anything at all in the world as funny. They are one of the few fanatical movements for which I am able to have any respect whatever."]

When useful, Merton says, the native is "humored and kidded along." But they learn that the whites have one kind of truth for the natives and another kind of truth for themselves. The native is treated as a "non-person."

What is going on everywhere is "a common drive towards identification, realization of one's dignity and assertion of one's rights as a human being." The Western world cannot crush the indigenous heroes: When Che Guevara was killed and his death was broadcast to the world as marking the end of a dangerous man, all that happened was "to raise him immediately to the status of a charismatic figure in the eyes of the Third World." And in another area: "With all our immense technological skill and all the tremendous versatility of destructive weapons . . . the Vietnam struggle itself takes on mythical dimensions of an absolutely disastrous character for America." What is created is "the mythdream of resistance fighters in a small minority asserting their identity and dignity as human beings against the marshalling of an enormous technological machine by the richest country in the world." He adds that "the white mythdream of absolute white supremacy is something that brooks no opposition," and he speaks of the "inner paranoid policing of the white man's own mind." What he said he was trying to do in this study of Cargo was "not just to discover something curious and exotic, but to reach the heart of our problems, our universal problem of communication. Our communication with primitives and with the primitive society demands an ability to communicate also with something deeper *in ourselves,* something with which we are out of touch. . . . We are out of contact with our own depths. It is our own primitive self which has become alien, hostile and strange."

One of his friends called Merton "a kind of free-lance monk" because he was growing so independent of the monastery. He constantly complained to friends that the Benedictine Rule was no longer being observed by the abbey in its original purity and that business considerations had taken the upper hand. He said once: "Was here a miracle woman, since reading Father Raymond she eats nothing but Trappist cheese exclusively, brought back from the gates of death by Trappist cheese." On another occasion: "There goes the whistle. Everybody into the fallout shelter and pack cheese." He sometimes recited a poem which began, "I think we should never freeze/Such lively assets as our cheese."

[Following page]

In his late forties, Merton began to worry about death. He wrote in his journal that "I think sometimes I may die soon, though I am not exactly old (forty-seven)." But later he said, "These years when you approach fifty and get ready to turn the corner are supposed to be the best in your life." He was then experiencing deep upheavals of "impatience, resentment, disgust." Yet he felt he was at the same time a "joyful" person. Though he thought he had nothing to complain of, an "unexpected chill comes out of the depths: and I breathe the cold air of darkness, the sense of void."

"Everybody suspects you," she says. "You are being followed, now. I wonder why they have not arrested you already."

OUR LAST MEETING. It was early in September 1968. During the summer Merton had written me saying he was planning on going to Asia, but it was a secret and not to tell anyone. In August I drove across America, through the rolling Midwest, and then across the flat cornfields of the great plains, across the mountains to Salt Lake City, and then south to New Mexico. In Abiquiu I visited some mutual friends, who told me the news that Merton was going to Asia but it was a secret. I headed East again; in Louisville I had a story to do, and here some people who were in contact with Gethsemani again told me about the trip, swearing me to secrecy. When I met Merton he assured me that "no one knows I'm going except the Abbot and one or two other people." Later I learned also that at the fifth annual conference of PAX, a peace association of which Merton was one of the sponsors, held at the Catholic Worker farm in Tivoli, New York, in July, Dorothy Day had announced that Merton was going to the Far East. At any rate, he told me that "Father Abbot will inform the community after I've left."

We walked about the woods and around the lake, where he used to stroll in meditation. He showed me a gnarled tree stump he had photographed for *Monk's Pond*, the quarterly he had published for a year; we came across a statue of St. Benedict which had been given to the monastery, but not being of exceptional quality, was removed into the forest where it served as a perch for the birds. We had several meals together in his hermitage, where we talked about past and present, and particularly about the coming trip. Merton was concerned about his finances. He was being given money for his ticket and for a few months, but beyond that he didn't know what he would do. He hoped that he could earn enough money by writing to keep himself going. In my mind I wondered how a man who had made so much money for the abbey and had been so much responsible for its well-being and

success could be treated so niggardly. I don't know if his fears signified a failure of communication with the new abbot, or if there was merely an attempt to keep him under control. I decided not to ask him about the immense royalties he had earned, which were said to have been turned over to the monastery without question, nor why he didn't have some small rights to the money when necessary. I thought it was none of my business and remained quiet.

My strongest impression at the time— and he said it quite clearly, too—was that he did not intend to return to Gethsemani. One of his fellow monks, in a magazine article later on, made the contradictory point emphatically to try to set the rumors aside. He quotes Merton as saying a few hours before his death, "I am a monk. I shall remain a monk until death. Nothing can stop me from being one." Earlier he had written to his community, while he was still in California, "I hope there are not too many crazy rumors. Keep telling everyone that I am a monk of Gethsemani and intend to remain one all my days." But he could have remained a monk of Gethsemani without ever seeing the monastery again. However, in the light of what happened, I am firmly convinced now that not only did he *not* intend on returning "home" but that he knew he was going to die abroad and perhaps in Asia. Before he left, he established a trust to care for his papers, and he is said to have written three "farewell" letters to close friends (all of them women); in one of them he gave instructions about burial. The feeling remains with me, clear and definite: He had completed his life within the monastery walls, a total of twenty-seven years, and the next twenty-seven would be spent in another milieu. I don't know the details of his relations with the new abbot, but my impression is that if, and when, Merton had written, from the Himalayas or from Thailand or Japan or wherever he decided to settle down, that he wanted to be a hermit *there*, permission would have been granted.

Merton expounded at length about his plans to
stay in Asia. Then right before he left
Gethsemani, he was visited by Dom Jean
LeClerq, a Belgian Benedictine he was to meet
in Bangkok. The two monks talked about the
coming conference and exchanged small talk
[next page].

We talked a lot about the East. I showed him a number of photographs I had taken in Asia, mainly in India, and he was moved and silent over the tragedy in them. Then he exploded with his usual enthusiasm, "Boy, some photographs!" We talked a long time about recent events and our personal lives. He was distressed because when he had made some telephone calls from the monastery, a lay brother had listened in and had reported the content to the abbot. Most of all he talked about Asia, the ordinary living problems of food and water and keeping well (he was worried about his stomach, which was still a serious medical problem), but he talked too about the Buddhist holy men he would be seeing. He spoke for a moment about the Tibetan *Book of the Dead*, which had become one of his special interests. "Boy, those Tibetans, they're way out." I remarked rather casually that the *Book of the Dead* was a big hippy fad and that Buddhist scholars had dismissed it as a serious work. He said they were crazy, they didn't know what they were talking about.

Two days after our parting, Merton left for the West Coast. He spent eight days in Santa Barbara, where he addressed the Center for the Study of Democratic Institutions, and then went up the coast to Whitehorn, to spend two days at Our Lady of the Redwoods Monastery. Then he began his trip to Asia. He had a few days in Bangkok, which he was to return to in December, then he began traveling about India. His first stop was Calcutta, where he was moved by the poverty he saw about him, poverty such as he had never seen before, even in Harlem during his Columbia days, and which is hard to imagine, poverty of such crushing cruelty that the average Westerner prefers to cut and run when he encounters it. Then he began his search into the roots of Buddhism, with trips to the Dalai Lama in the Himalayas, and to colonies of Tibetan refugees in Darjeeling, in northeastern India. The Dalai Lama lives in Dharmsala, an overnight train trip from New Delhi. Here Merton spent eight days, in a kind of retreat, reading and meditating and meeting Tibetan masters. He had three long interviews with the Dalai Lama, and endless talks with other monks.

Merton found the Dalai Lama "very alert and energetic . . . simple and outgoing." The Dalai Lama spoke to him with great openness and frankness: "He is in no sense what you would expect of a political emigré and the things he said about Communism seemed to me fair and objective. His real interests are monastic and mystical." Merton then added: "We spoke almost entirely about the life of meditation, about *samadhi* (concentration), which is the first stage of meditative discipline and where one systematically clarifies and recollects his mind." He points out that "The Tibetans have a very acute, subtle and scientific knowledge of 'the mind.'" The two monks then discussed the higher forms of prayer, and Tibetan mysticism, most of which is esoteric and is kept strictly secret, and compared Tibetan mysticism to Zen. "In either case," said Merton, "the highest mysticism is in some ways quite 'simple'— but always and everywhere the Dalai Lama kept insisting on the fact that one could not attain anything in the spiritual life without total dedication, continued effort, experienced guidance, real discipline, and the combination of wisdom and method (which is stressed by Tibetan mysticism)." The Dalai Lama questioned Merton about Western monasticism—whether Christian monks, by their vows, were committed to a "high attainment" and constituted an initiation into a mystical tradition and experience under a qualified master. The Lama wanted to know "what kind of attainment the monks might achieve and if there were possibilities of a deep mystical life in our monasteries." Merton, being a realist and always a little bit cynical, remarked, "Well, that is what they are supposed to be for, but many monks seem to be interested in something else."

On one of his walks in the woods, he clowned
about with a statue of St. Benedict which had
been exiled. Two days later he was on his way
across America in the first stage of his Asian
journey.

At Darjeeling, Merton met many other Tibetans who impressed him with their mystical attainment; some were lay people who were very far advanced in a special type of Tibetan contemplation which resembles Zen and is called Dzogtchen. And here, in the encounter with these very deep and knowledgeable and disciplined Tibetans, he began to realize, as he informed Bob Lax only half-jokingly, he began to get the idea that they considered him more than a wise man from the West. To them he was a Buddha. Earlier he had warned, in an essay titled "Transcendent Experience," "It becomes overwhelmingly important for us *to become detached from our everyday conception of ourselves as potential subjects for special and unique experiences, or as candidates for realization, attainment and fulfillment* [the italics are his]. In other words, this means that a spiritual guide worth his salt will conduct a ruthless campaign against all forms of delusion arising out of a spiritual ambition and self-complacency which aim to establish the ego in spiritual glory. That is why a St. John of the Cross is so hostile to visions, ecstasies and all forms of 'special experience.' That is why the Zen Masters say: 'If you meet the Buddha, kill him.' "

*

FROM DARJEELING, which like Dharmsala is on the edge of the Himalayas (one can see Mount Everest in the distance in good weather), Merton hoped to go to Sikkim, another important Buddhist country. He expected to visit the Karmapa Lama, who had established a new center at Rumtek. Even under good conditions, Rumtek is five hours from Darjeeling through treacherous mountain roads, with unguarded, sheer drops on one side or the other of the narrow roads, but the bridge over the Tista River was washed out by landslides which had been caused by heavy rains and floods. While he was waiting for news about the passage into Sikkim, Merton had a long

series of talks with a Tibetan monk from another tradition than that of the Dalai Lama. This man was a spiritual master (I have been unable to learn his name, which is possibly irrelevant anyway) of Dzogtchen ("Great Accomplishment"), the initiatic family which is a branch of the Nyingmapa ("Order of Ancients"), the original form of Buddhism in Tibet. (The Dalai Lama belongs to the Gelugpa, or "Order of Virtuous Usage," a reformed movement which developed much later.) The Nyingmapa is a more relaxed, open and unreformed order which has given a great number of Tibetan saints to the world (and also sinners, because of its relatively unstructured form). It was here, among these Dzogtchen Tibetan Buddhists, that Merton got the opportunity to go out into the jungle forest on the steep hills and live for four days as a Buddhist recluse in deep meditation. And from what I was told later in my talks with a medium who had spoken to Merton, it was during this period in the jungle, that Merton spoke directly with the Gautama Buddha. I will return to this very touchy and controversial event shortly, but what had happened was that Merton had an experience which transcended time, space and reality. I think at this point he must have realized how far he had come up the seven storey mountain; his ascent had reached its climax, unexpectedly, in a mountain jungle on the edge of the Himalayas.

When he got down to Calcutta again, there were two great Hindu festivals going on. One was the celebration of Diwali, the festival of lights, during which an immense number of firecrackers are set off, and the other, the offering of puja, or worship, to the goddess Kali, the great creator and destroyer, who is particularly loved by the Bengalis. The Bengalis make clay images, often several times life-size, which are painted blue and installed in beautifully delicate bamboo and paper shrines all over Calcutta and the countryside. Kali's eyes are fierce with excitement: she wears a necklace of skulls, and her tongue is sticking out, and she is trampling on her husband, Shiva. In the company of "an escaped lama" Merton bought fireworks to celebrate Diwali; he remarked, too, that Kali can come to America and trample on some husbands, starting with Mayor Daley and Governor Wallace. Then he attended the immersion ceremonies for Kali; on the third night of her puja, the images are taken to the Hooghly, an offshoot of the Ganges, in torchlight processions to the accompaniment of drums and cymbals, and immersed in the muddy waters. The images melt away, and Kali is no more.

Merton told people he was "crazy about Calcutta." He tried unsuccessfully to locate Bramachari, who has an ashram or monastery on the outskirts of Calcutta. However, Bramachari, who was born in what is now East Pakistan, has not been able to cross the border into India, and he has not visited the ashram since 1965. Merton said Mass in the home of an American family, the Flanagans, who had been taking care of his mail; earlier, on his first passage through Calcutta, he participated in a meeting of the World Conference of Religions, at which Hindus, Sikhs, Jews, Muslims, Buddhists, Jains and Christians each spoke about their respective faiths in the context of a world encounter. "I come as a pilgrim who is anxious to obtain not just information," Merton said to this tremendous gathering, which was basically Eastern, "not just 'facts' about other monastic traditions, but to drink from ancient sources of monastic vision and experience." He expressed the belief that there was a real possibility of contact on a deep level between the contemplative and monastic tradition of the West and the various contemplative traditions in the East. He specifically mentioned the Sufis of Islam, the mystical lay-contemplative societies in Indonesia, along with the better known monastic groups in Hinduism and Buddhism. "Without asserting that there is a complete unity of all religions at the 'top,' at the transcendent or mystical level—since they all start from different dogmatic positions to 'meet' at this summit—it is certainly true to say that even where there are irreconcilable differences in doctrine and in formulated belief, there may still be great similarities and analogies in the realm of religious experience. There is nothing new in the observation that holy men like St. Francis and Sri Ramakrishna (to mention only two) have attained to a level of spiritual fulfillment which is at once universally recognizable and relevant to anyone interested in the religious dimension of experience. Cultural and doctrinal differences must remain, but they do not invalidate a very real quality of existential likeness."

What struck several people at the conference was that Merton seemed transcended. "No matter how much you talked to him, you got the feeling that he was always apart," said one participant. Another remarked that he seemed unsettled. At Gethsemani I had noticed this too. I had ascribed his appearance of being in another world to the tensions posed by his trip. Bob Lax, who had seen him earlier in the summer made the same observation; I told Lax that I thought the Old Boy (which was what we called him) wasn't relating to people; Lax agreed. Now, I wonder if he was not literally in another world.

*

"If you meet the Buddha, kill him."

ZEN SAYING

THERE WAS a lot that wasn't clear the last few years. He was encompassing more than people could absorb. It was as if he was trying to pack every idea he ever had —and every experience—into a year or two. His last abbot said in the funeral homily: "The possibility of death was not absent from his mind. We spoke of this before he set out—first jokingly, then seriously. He was ready for it. He even saw a certain fittingness in dying over there amidst those Asian monks [he meant, apparently, the Buddhists] who symbolized for him man's ancient and perennial desire for the deep things of God." But for years before this particular conversation, he had been foreseeing his death: In 1962, he wrote in his journal, "I think that I may soon die, though I am not yet old (forty-seven)." Three years later he wrote to a sister, "I am now pushing fifty and realize more and more that every extra day is just a free gift." (A month earlier he had officially become a hermit.) I think he felt that he had lost contact with a large part of the world with which he had previously been in touch. People were turned away by his interest in Buddhism. (One man in a typical statement said afterward that he considered Merton's works on Zen "an esoteric or eccentric pastime." In another case, a writer, who had spent eleven of twenty-two pages of an article discussing Merton's Buddhism, found all eleven deleted and material on Merton's early girl friends substituted by his editor.) His life, outwardly calm and in full accord with his own long-expressed wishes, was deepening, but I suspect it was also earning some new tensions. He had always been accustomed to running along the edge of the precipice, to living marginally. During the beat period he had identified himself with the beats, and when the hippies replaced them, with the hippies. He once remarked that the monk (he meant himself, of course, and not the usual timeservers in most monasteries) was among the marginal persons who lived in the presence of death, like prisoners and displaced people, in an act which calls into question the meaning of life. And then, he had always been a man of tremendous natural energies and appetites, he had, apparently, come full circle to certain passions of his teens and college years. His life was becoming more complicated and complex, and the tensions increased.

At the Bangkok meeting, where he delivered a talk entitled "Marxism and Monastic Perspectives," the day of his death (he was very much interested in Herbert Marcuse, and felt that both monasticism and Communism have certain things in common, among them a critical attitude toward established social and personal structures and a drive toward change), he also made some strong statements about celibacy. The day previous to his death he had translated for a French monk and then led the following discussion. He was interested, he said, in the Buddhist custom of having married monks. (He once remarked to me that "If I ever get married, it would be to an Indian woman.") An American participant intervened with the objection that in his opinion a completely chaste life was necessary for the highest mystical experience. But Merton (and some others) implied that conditions had changed, and that celibacy, even for the monk, was a thing of the past.

*

THUS HE WAS inevitably led out of the monastery, just as years earlier he had been inevitably led into it. He had already

made a number of shorter trips throughout the United States, to meetings and conferences, to New York to see Dr. D. T. Suzuki, the Zen Buddhist scholar with whom he engaged in a dialogue that evaluated the similarities and the differences between Zen and Christianity, and to visit certain other monastic foundations. His health had never been good; life was almost unbearable at times. There were many stays in the hospital in Louisville, and constant trips to the doctors. In the big cities, and on planes and trains and buses he saw what was happening to the world; he read newspapers and books, and went to the movies (he thought *What's New, Pussycat* very funny). He had an endless amount of correspondence with people all over the world, not only with the great and the famous, with scholars and intellectuals, but with the unknown, with ordinary people who wrote him out of appreciation, or anger or despair and loneliness. The trip to Asia had been on his mind a long, long time. On the surface, and this was the announced purpose, he was visiting Trappist foundations in Asia, but his real reason was to plunge deep into the wellsprings of Eastern mysticism, Buddhism above all. His search for Buddhism ran not only like an undercurrent throughout the years after his ordination, but at the end, like a torrent. And he knew with sorrow that while he was searching for the mystical, nonviolent path of the East, he would at the same time see human suffering at its

Dr. Bramachari, Merton's close friend from Columbia, had expected to see him again in Calcutta. Bramachari lives in East Pakistan but is unable to cross the border into India. He is now a wandering monk, visiting tiny and obscure Hindu communities in East Bengal, practicing the kind of nomadic religious life that had appealed strongly to Merton. Here Bramachari is holding a copy of the photograph of Lord Jagad-Bondhu.

rawest, most hopeless, and that this too could be the source of searingly polemical writings of the future. The gates of Gethsemani had closed behind him: like the Count of Monte Cristo, he had cut himself out of the sack. After his firsthand experiences with Buddhist mysticism in India, he returned to Bangkok for the advertised conference with Benedictine and Trappist monks on the future of the monastic life in Asia. It was here, in a suburb, that the terrible accident happened; the savage electrical flash that charred his skin and stopped his heart. Merton had once written a friend that "The scenario calls for a quiet death among concerned chipmunks," a news magazine reported in its obituary, "and I'd like it that way." But in the strange insight he possessed, he had earlier foreshadowed his final moments. I wonder how many people have gone back again to *The Seven Storey Mountain?* The last few pages are particularly interesting, where Merton concludes with a fine meditative passage, in which he imagines God speaking to him about his long journey and then his dying, first in the spirit and then in the flesh. "And when you have been praised a little and loved a little I will take away all your gifts and all your love and all your praise and you will be utterly forgotten and abandoned and you will be nothing, a dead thing, a rejection. And in that day you shall begin to possess the solitude you have so long desired. And your solitude will bear immense fruit in the souls of men you will never see on earth.

"Do not ask when it will be or where it will be or how it will be: On a mountain or in a prison, in a desert or in a concentration camp or in a hospital or at Gethsemani. It does not matter. So do not ask me, because I am not going to tell you. You will not know until you are in it."

And then there is that final, devastating line:

"That you may become the brother of God and learn to know the Christ of the burnt men."

AND WHAT of the end? I had just returned from a trip to New England, which was accomplished in frightful cold and discomfort. I had an accident on the expressway coming into New York, and was forced to abandon my car temporarily and return home to telephone for help. While I was trying to reach a garage, a call came from a friend in the peace movement, who apologized for being the first to give me such disquieting news, but Thomas Merton was dead. I turned on a news broadcast, and there was a brief announcement, frustrating because of the lack of information at that time. I returned to my car—it was then two A.M.—and while standing there on the highway in the bitter cold, amid the fluorescent lights and the plunging machines that roared by like so many rocket ships, I thought about death. John Paul, Williams, Bob Mack, Joe H., Gerdy, Slate, Reinhardt, Freedgood had already died. Plus all the others who had passed around the periphery of our lives, and the people who had freaked out, like Harry R., who had been found by Seymour one morning wandering barefoot in Central Park wearing only his pajama bottoms. I had almost been killed —my car had hit an abutment; a few inches further to the right would have flipped it over—but Merton *was* dead, mysteriously, secretly. "It is difficult to determine at this stage just exactly what was the cause of his death," said the six Trappist delegates to the conference in a jointly signed letter to the abbot of Gethsemani. They added, "In death Father Louis's face was set in a great and deep peace and it was obvious that he had found Him Whom he had searched for so diligently."

*

ADOLPH PAGANUZZI, a pastry chef, once said to me, "If Merton should die, I would not hesitate to pray to him as a saint."

*

A NICE LADY, who handled many of his business affairs, said in a lecture after his death that she often argued with him. She said she ultimately realized that "his holiness was much better than the holiness I tried to force on him." We can imagine her frustrations.

*

THE TIBETAN BOOK OF THE DEAD. "The Bardo Thödol [Book of the Dead] offers one an intelligible philosophy addressed to human beings rather than to gods or primitive savages.... [It is in part] an initiation process whose purpose is to restore to the soul the divinity it lost at birth.... It is a primordial, universal idea that the dead simply continue their earthly existence and do not know that they are disembodied spirits—an archetypal idea which enters into immediate, visible manifestation whenever anyone sees a ghost.... The Bardol Thödol began by being a 'closed' book, and so it has remained, no matter what kind of commentaries may be written upon it. For it is a book that will open itself only to spiritual understanding, and this is the capacity which no man is born with, but which he can only acquire through special training and special experience. It is good that such to all intents and purposes 'useless' books exist. They are meant for those 'queer folk' who no longer set much store by the uses, aims and meaning of present-day 'civilisation.'" (Dr. C. G. Jung, *Das Tibetanische Totenbuch.*)

*

THE NEXT TWO items are reported merely for the record. After all, the reader is a modern skeptic, as I am. (We don't even believe in the Little Flower, do we?)

In New Canaan, Connecticut, a Protestant minister, who is also a medium, said that Merton came to him shortly after his death. The minister remarked, "I had never read Merton, I didn't know he had died, I hardly knew who he was. But what he told me of the details of his death were exactly the same as those described in the letter the Trappist delegates wrote." Merton told the minister that he had not committed suicide, though he had knowingly touched the live wire in a subconscious wish to join the Infinite. "I spent too much time looking in the wrong place," said Merton. "I should have looked within."

Medium Number Two receives his messages on a barge in the river between Staten Island and New Jersey. "I spoke to Master Thomas," he told me. "That is what he is now called. He is also known as Master Davog and Master B. E. Merton is in Shigatze, Tibet; the Chinese are giving him a hard time. Merton still retains his body; he has reached the Eighth Initiation. He has had his last incarnation. Previously he was incarnated as a Presbyterian minister named Dag Bead in Sweden. He lived from 1634 to 1654 and died of frostbite in Iceland where he went as a missionary. His body is no longer in Gethsemani; if you looked there, you'd find an empty grave. His body has been transmuted because he is ascended. He's beyond physical death. If you saw him now, he would look better than you had seen him before. Radiant. Master Thomas's role now is to prepare for the Second Coming of Jesus, which will happen in 2040 A.D."

*

AN EASTERN LADY wanted to know what I had been working on so diligently. I replied that I was writing a book about an Englishman who became a Communist, then a Catholic, later a Trappist monk, and finally a Buddhist, at which point, his life having been fulfilled, he died.

An American businessman asked the same question. I replied that I was writing a biography of a fellow who had made a million or two as a writer but gave the money to a religious order. "Must have been crazy," said the businessman.

*

I ASKED an astrologer (a highly gifted, perceptive nonprofessional) to draw up Merton's horoscope. He was born on January 31, 1915, as you will recall. Here are excerpts from the report:

"A conglomorate of planets in Aquarius. Mars leads the parade in 0° of Aquarius and Jupiter ends it in the last (the astrologically fateful 29th degree). Within this highly strategic, concentrated area (a mere thirty degrees) out of a whole, complete, beautiful circle of 360 are two sets of near partile (exact) conjunctions: sun and Uranus, Mercury and Jupiter. The moon, which together with the sun and ascendant forms the trilogy nucleus of everything the person is, is in close and powerful opposition to the stellium in Aquarius, makes this the most Aquarian planetary pattern I have ever seen: something like a dozen or more atom bombs pitchforked onto an area one third the size of Hiroshima. Saturn (retrograde), the karmic planet is in Gemini, also relating to 'mind.' Aquarius: abstracted, conceptual life, detachment, the will to be free, thinking in universal terms. Its ruler, Uranus, historically associated with revolution: a mind thing in the first place. Venus: gentleness, love in its Christ form (as distinct from sexual love) in Sagittarius, the sign of the clergy (among other things) is in harmonious relationship (sextile) to the Aquarian stellium and as well to the moon (trine). This all suggests a fantastically powerful concentration of mind-soul. I would say that this man was something of an anachronism, living perhaps a century ahead of his time, a prophet, a symbol of what will be."

*

Alligator.
Black dog.
Thomas Merton.
Incarnate Buddha.
The ten thousand names of Buddha.
Master Thomas.

*

A hippy said to me: "Did he give out good vibrations?" "Yes," I said, "he did."

"There is another side to the mountain."

EPILOGUE

THE MAN IN THE SYCAMORE TREE MEETS THE LORD BUDDHA

DEAD ... but in the brief decades that have followed the tragedy in Bangkok he seems very much alive, very much—and the mysteries proliferate. "I am going home, to the home where I have never been in this body," Merton had written in his journal as his plane set out across the Pacific. A home where I have never been in this body—a very oriental concept, common among Hindus, Buddhists, and certain Sufis. Unlike the West, where the body "gives up the ghost" at death, in the East the soul sheds that useless appendage, the body. And the soul has been "everywhere." Merton had also written in his journal, "May I never come back without having settled the great affair. And found also the great compassion, mahakaruna." Mahakaruna, the "saving grace" the Buddhas show toward all mortal beings. Merton had wanted "to go to the country beyond words and beyond reason." If only we had better clues to his thoughts on that fated trip.

*

HIS DEATH UNLOCKED at least some secret doors of the distant past. The vaguely hinted-at story of the woman and the child—Merton's son—is now somewhat clearer, but still not fully explained. That they were the "impediment" that led the Franciscans to reject him is more than likely. But they were not an impediment to the Trappists. The woman (we now hear of girls named Joan and Sylvia, and they have thus become real and alive rather than an abstraction) and the child (whose name is still unknown) were very much a concern during Merton's Columbia days and his early years as a Cistercian, which suggests he carried a heavy spiritual and psychological burden, for he was a man of compassion with an overwhelming sense of "sinfulness." Merton's closest friends believed that the woman and the boy died during the German air raids on Britain, some seven or eight years after his guardian learned of the affair and banished him from England into exile in America. Had he lived, the boy would be middle-aged

today. We might wonder about him— what he would have been like, the son of a father famous as a monk and a writer. Would he, too, have been a writer or an artist (or even a monk like his father)?

The fate of Merton's son is a faraway issue. Answers to other, less remote questions are slowly emerging as various documents are released by his Order and as biographers, scholars, academics, and popularizers probe into hitherto restricted papers, journals, letters, and unpublished manuscripts, lending new perspective to published writings. We can now make a better, yet far from complete assessment of Merton—one still somewhat in the realm of speculation. That Merton was a saint many might question (his younger brother, John Paul, is a better candidate). More clearly, Merton was one of the rare, self-taught spiritual masters who appear spontaneously, without antecedent. The Sufis call such a person a "qalandar," a type of religious individual, whom Captain Sir Richard Francis Burton has said "works out his salvation by himself." Because of their free-ranging activities qalandars have come under criticism (one modern academic calls them "Islamic beatniks," a term Merton would have enjoyed), but Burton states that the movement "has produced some very distinguished saints." In a better known term, Merton was a type of guru, still self-taught and without a traditional master, but one of a line of teachers that goes back to the mists of antiquity, possessing the knowledge ("gnosis") and insights denied lesser men, though they may have had years of training. (Monsignor Jodot, the apostolic nuncio for southeast Asia at the time of Merton's death, has remarked that to him Merton was a true guru; that he had "the charisma of a guru.") In oriental terms one receives "darshan," vision, a spiritual blessing by the mere presence of a guru, something often noted by those who met Merton. One might also place Merton among the "prophets" in a classical sense, a man "sent" to speak of the oneness of All

Being, in Merton's case, to Christians, Buddhists, Hindus, Muslims; to pagans, animists, atheists—to whoever will listen. (Jodot again: "To me he is a kind of prophet [who] reopened old ways we had forgotten.") More than ever before we see that his very presence was strengthened—fortified—by earth-shaking encounters which are just being recognized in current assessments.

Signposts, markers, even flares and rockets appeared all along his path. In Cuba, in the spring of 1940 (during the trip for which he decorated his passport photograph with a beard), he had gone into a simple parish church in Havana for Mass. There something inexplicable happened:

> Something went off inside me like a thunderclap and without saying or apprehending anything extraordinary through any of my senses . . . I knew with the most absolute and unquestionable certainty that before me . . . [was] God in all His essence, all His power, all His glory, and God in Himself . . . the unshakable certainty, the clear and immediate knowledge . . . struck me like a thunderbolt and went through me like a flash of lightning and seemed to lift me clean up off the earth.

Few Christian mystics ever write about their experiences (Muslims are more likely to, but then, theirs is a different tradition), and those who do are traditionally very cautious about what they say. This passage, written in a then private journal, seems to conform to traditional patterns of mystical experience. Such experiences were not unfamiliar to Merton—"It was in no way an extraordinary kind of experience, but only one that had greater intensity than I had experienced before," he wrote in his journal.

Here and there other clues emerge to indicate the kind of inner life he enjoyed—some clear, some shadowy pointers to a deepening and increasingly intense absorption into the Divine. Once he referred obliquely to "my bloody mysticism." In 1958 he had an interesting exchange of letters with Aldous Huxley, who favored the use of certain drugs, especially mescaline and lysergic acid, to lead to mystical experience in those already prepared for it. Merton, writing out of what seemed to be personal knowledge, said that "a fully mystical experience had in its very essence some note of direct spiritual contact of two liberties, a kind of flash or spark which ignites an intuition of all that has been said above [in the beginning of his letter], plus something more which I can only describe as 'personal,' in which God is known not as an 'object' or as 'in up there' or 'him in everything' nor as 'the All' but as—the Biblical expression—I AM, or simply AM. . . . It is a presence of a Person and depends on the liberty of that Person. . . ." He also spoke of "an experience of 'oneness' within oneself . . . a flash of awareness of the transcendent Reality that is within all that is real. . . ."

A few years later (in The New Man) he spoke of "the clear inebriation of mysticism," a tantalizing statement that cries out for explanation and elucidation. What did he mean? Was he blessed with the transports of John of the Cross and of Teresa of Avila, two saints of immense appeal during his Columbia days?

A further revelation comes in a letter to a Sufi, Aziz Shaykh Abdul, an Algerian, to whom Merton was writing about his daily life, which was quite close to that of the members of the Muslim brotherhoods. Here Merton took the rare step of talking about his own spiritual practices ("I do not ordinarily write about such things," he remarked). His prayer was "centered entirely on attention to the presence of God and to His will and His love. . . . One might say this gives my meditation the character described by the Prophet [Muhammad] as 'being before God as if you saw Him'. . . . My prayer tends very much to what you [the Sufis] call fanā." Merton said he was not "thinking about" anything, but his prayer is "a direct seeking of the Face of the Invisible, which cannot be found unless we become lost in Him who is invisible."

Such a method of prayer and meditation is unusual in ordinary monastic practice but not among Sufis. And if Merton had attained *fanā* he had indeed reached extraordinary spiritual heights, for according to the Sufi manual, the *'Awārif-u'l-Ma'ārif*, *fanā* is "the end of travelling to God." It is "the thinking away of Self," and is "the prayer of rapture, wherein man is effaced from self." "The highest state is to be effaced from effacement," the manual adds, quoting from the *Gulshan-i-Raz*, another basic Sufi work. The great Algerian master, the late Aḥmad al-'Alawī, whose family and spiritual geneaology go directly back to Muhammad and whose namesake was one of Merton's friends and correspondents, preached especially what Merton sought: the Oneness of Being and meditation on the Holy Face, a doctrine often found in the Qur'an: "Wherever ye turn, there is the Face of God.... Everything shall perish but His Face...."

There were other Sufis, Algerians, with whom Merton had some connection (either in person or by letter) during his last years at Gethsemani, who recognized in him a soul "on the verge of some important spiritual union." Sidi Abdeslam, who counselled Merton that "what is best is what is not said [about spiritual matters]," predicted that Abbot James, with whom Merton had so many disagreements over the years, would either die or retire in 1968 and that Merton would be able to travel. The younger Aḥmad al-'Alawī offered Merton a refuge in Algeria—"It seems that I have a living place in a living and secret tradition," noted Merton. The term "secret" is an interesting qualification, for by that time Merton seems to have fully entered a kind of "gnostic" involvement.

*

ABBOT JAMES RETIRED as predicted, and so came the fateful, inevitable trip to Asia. The famous interviews with the Dalai Lama brought him face to face with the very heart of a certain kind of Buddhism. In isolation at Darjeeling, among another group of Tibetans, Merton seems to have had a particularly intense spiritual encounter, to which I referred earlier. But there was more. Like the Algerians, the Tibetans recognized Merton as someone in an advanced spiritual state, calling him a "ranjung Sangay," a natural Buddha. One of the Tibetans told Merton that he was "on the edge of great realization." His journals during this period record strange dreams. In one he returned to Gethsemani dressed as a Tibetan, "a kind of Zen monk and Gelugpa together." In another dream about the great Himalayan peak Kanchenjunga, a voice told him, "There is another side to the mountain," perhaps meaning that he should see the world from the Tibetan point of view. On his way down to Calcutta he met a young Australian, who observed that Merton had "that 'washed' face only those . . . who have just been through an LSD experience of some major mystic dimension [have]." It was not likely that Merton had taken any sort of hallucinogen. The Australian emphasized that Merton had "that clearer than clean, serenely open, quite halo-like face that I only saw on people after [they had had] a deeply moving psychedelic experience. . . ." In south India his visit to the great shrine of Mahablipuram, a kind of Hindu Seven Storey Mountain, brought an interior experience he vaguely hinted at a few days later in his journal, after he had visited the Buddhist shrine at Polonnaruwa in Sri Lanka. Here his experience was quite reminiscent of that in the church in Havana, almost three decades earlier. He approached the Buddhas "barefoot and undisturbed, my feet in wet grass, wet sand. . . . Then all the silence of the extraordinary faces. The great smiles. Huge and yet subtle. Filled with every possibility, questioning nothing, knowing everything, rejecting nothing. . . . Looking at these figures I was suddenly, almost forcibly, jerked clean out of the habitual half-tied vision of things, and an inner clearness, clarity, as if exploding from the rocks themselves,

became evident and obvious. . . . I know
and have seen what I was obscurely
looking for. I don't know what else
remains but I have now seen and pierced
through the surface and gotten beyond
the shadow and the disguise."

*

HE HAD SEVERAL times said he wanted to
"disappear," though his remark at the end
of his speech at Bangkok—"So I will
disappear"—seems to be a hagiographer's
addition to the published text. However,
after he had left Polonnaruwa he asked,
"What if the mind becomes one-pointed /
And the 'one point' is then removed?"
And finally, "Where do you go from the
top of a thirty-foot pole?" His long
attachment to Zen, which his critics have
treated with so much suspicion and even
disdain, seems in retrospect an attempt
"to get the self out of the Self," an echo
of the words of the great Rhenish mystic
Jacob Boehme, to "cease from the
thinking of self and the willing of self."
Only then, with the mirror of the soul
wiped clean, can the effacing of
effacement be achieved.

Merton became more and more "oriental" in his appearance, as in his thinking and writing. Here, not long before the trip to Asia, Lax has photographed Merton very much the laughing Buddha.

"*I am carried away by the
same wind
that blows all these people
down the street,
like pieces of paper
and
        dead leaves
in all
        directions.*"